Clocking In

Ralph Capenerhurst was born and brought up in Derby. He worked for thirty-three years in a British Rail workshop, where he became shop steward, before going to St John's Theological College in Nottingham. He is now back in his home town and working as an industrial chaplain.

Author of two other books and well known for the many years he wrote a regular column for *Today* magazine, Ralph Capenerhurst is married with two grown up daughters and a grandson.

Ralph Capenerhurst

Clocking In

Revelations of a shop steward turned
industrial chaplain

First published 1987
Triangle
SPCK
Holy Trinity Church
Marylebone Road
London NW1 4DU

British Library Cataloguing in Publication Data

Capenerhurst, Ralph
  Clocking In: Revelations of a shop steward
  turned industrial chaplain.
  1. Capenerhurst, Ralph   2. Church of
  England——Clergy——Biography
  I. Title
  283'.092'4   BX5199.C/

  ISBN 0-281-04250-0

Photoset by Hart-Talbot Printers Ltd,
Saffron Walden, Essex
Printed in Great Britain by
Hazell, Watson & Viney Limited
Member of the BPCC Group
Aylesbury, Bucks

For Pat

Contents

Contents

1

Initiation

I became a shop steward primarily because nobody else wanted the job. The supplies department of the British Rail Works employed one hundred-odd blokes who were apathetic towards any kind of union involvement (unless there was some cash or holidays at the end of the line) and because I had the reputation of having the 'gift of the gab' I was asked to stand for election.

I felt a bit like Moses when he was told by God to lead the children of Israel out of Egypt; my particular Israelites were the kind who wanted their milk and honey pre-packaged with handling-money payable at time and a half.

'You'll be alright,' said the other shop steward and my future colleague, Ned. 'Just remember to get your facts straight before you get in the gaffer's office 'n always get a minuted meetin' on sticky points so as you can nail the gaffer at some future date.'

Ned, with his peaked cap, always reminded me of a St Bernard that had lost its barrel. His cheeks sagged and his eyes had a mournful look of quiet despair. Still, he knew the union rulebook and he was totally incorruptible to managerial blandishments. He could never be 'buttered up'.

The retiring steward was a colourless personality who was always suspected of being a Tory in overalls and, nearing the end of his three year stint, had felt secure enough to show his real colours. He had incurred the displeasure of the men by his declared intention to spend what little time he had left as the men's representative in overthrowing Socialism in the land.

So, having an election agent who made it his business to collect five signatures supporting my claim to be the elected representative of the men on the supplies department, I began the job of convincing myself, as well as everybody else, that I could do the job. One thing clearly emerged from the start. According to the men, management was, in the main, without known parentage, and out to cut the working man's wages at every point. The knight in shining armour was the dedicated shop steward who fought the dragon of vested managerial interest with a rule book fortified by working-class solidarity. There were accepted principles of negotiation, well-defined areas of understanding; motives were suspect and so both management and shop stewards began discussions from impossible positions. The strategy of both was to lay down a creeping barrage of goodwill until they met somewhere in the middle.

There were two other candidates for the position of shop steward, but both had obvious drawbacks. One spent a good deal of time 'knocking on the green door' – a derisory expression which meant he was a malingerer and afraid of honest work coupled with living off the proceeds of social security. The verdict of the men was that he was a social pariah. It was widely believed that the other chap had a relative in the higher echelons of the British Medical Association, judging by the number of certificated absences from his place of employment on medical grounds. It was pretty obvious that neither of these two characters could represent the men, so when election day arrived they were non-starters and I romped home with a whopping majority.

When the result was announced Ned said that I had to accompany him to the Works Committee office together with the defeated candidates. There, congratulations and commiserations would be doled out by the Secretary and Chairman of the Works Committee. The Works Committee was, in effect, the inner caucus of the shop stewards' negotiating machinery. Everything was very civilized. Sam Stodd, the Chairman, was fifty-ish and a very astute and dapper little man dressed in a dark lounge suit. He had piercing blue eyes, wore rimless spectacles and proudly sported his National Union of Railwaymen badge. His wide experience of industrial matters well-qualified him to be a general Urim and Thummin on most of the issues that arose in the Works. His partner, George Grundy, Secretary of the Committee, was a younger man – thin, hatchet-faced, articulate and even-tempered, and also well-grounded in industrial matters. He was dressed in a blue boiler suit which effectively earthed him with the men who had put him in office. Sam, on the other hand, had a passport to sartorial elegance by the fact that he had stood as an unsuccessful Labour candidate at the last general election; he had also spent three years in London seconded to the Executive Committee of the NUR, the all-important body which used to spend marathon sessions in wage negotiations and the art of brinkmanship at 10 Downing Street with Sir Harold Wilson, fortified with beer and sandwiches. Sam and George: two very level-headed and able men whose integrity I immediately respected.

Our meeting was quaintly formal. They first of all com-miserated with the losers: 'Hope this doesn't deter you chaps from putting up as shop representatives in the future. We hope you'll take a lively interest in Union affairs and we shall look forward to your continuing support.' There were a series of embarrassed grunts, a round of hand-shaking and then they turned to me.

'Congratulations' Sam said. 'We hope you have a suc-cessful term of office and we look forward to working with you.' More shaking of hands and the rather stiff little ceremony was concluded.

Ned and me walked away together. We had a lot in common, being the same age and having served in the same theatre of operations during the war. In 1947 we had entered the railway industry, and we shared a common experience in our trade as storekeepers.

'I'll be leaning on you for a bit,' I said thoughtfully to Ned.

He clicked his teeth and gave a smug, self-satisfied little smile. 'You'll get used to it. One thing's important though,' and he assumed a conspiratorial attitude, 'if the gaffer 'as us in the office, we must be in absolute agreement beforehand, otherwise, we've 'ad it. It doesn't matter what the discussion might be about – you name it, pay, conditions, discipline – we must never allow ourselves to be split on *any* issue!'

'Not even if we honestly disagree?'

'Disagree on owt you like mate – but not in there, get it?' and he jerked his thumb in the direction of the gaffer's office.

'Yes. I think I get it,' I replied, a little unsure.

'If you get stuck on anything, I mean, if the lads come to you with a *problem*, a real *problem* 'n you're stuck – just fetch me!'

I tried to think of all the problems I might get 'stuck' on. I thought of the hundred-odd characters in the department; the ones whose tempers had short fuses when they thought the Inland Revenue was defrauding them in the Friday wage packet; the men who regarded the shop steward as the vade-mecum of every aspect of British Rail's complex wage and bargaining structure; and those who saw a strike as the only solution to secure their 'rights'. Already, I smelt the bush-fires of discontent on the shop floor smouldering in my nostrils. As I parted from Ned he looked at me with his sad eyes. He seemed to have aged considerably in the last quarter of an hour.

'You're quite certain you're fitted for the job?' he enquired.

'Only time will tell Ned, only time will tell!' And my doubts began to emerge . . .

I later discovered that as a shop steward I had no defined terms of reference. I was a middleman, an all-purpose, all-seasons fixer; an industrial ombudsman who must recognize that management has certain equal rights as do the workers. But my role as the workers' representative was to ensure that their rights were *more* right than the management. I was the lubricant in the abrasive parts of the negotiating machinery – the sick-money collector, the 'official' representative at funerals, the watch dog on Westminster, and the interpreter of obscure documents re-grading the workers' pension rights . . . and so on.

I thought of the occasions when, during a shop floor debate in the tea break, I had passionately declared my opposition to the dirty face of capitalism; when I had blown a fair head of steam about the Swiss bankers and the blackmail that was just another way of describing a run on the pound. Unthinkingly, I had been laying down an expected course of action when I had taken verbal pot-shots at the Establishment and made bolshy statements about the Common Market con and work-ins. Little did I realize my strictures regarding Them and Us would finish up with me being at the head of the militant column. I had pontificated about Them having toilets and Us having lavatories; Us having a canteen and Them having a dining room; They had salaries while We had wages; They were paid monthly, We were paid weekly; They had careers and We had jobs; They signed in and We clocked in . . . In retrospect, I had been finding a refuge in my working class origins and this was totally at variance with my Christian witness.

I made plenty of mistakes during my first year in office. Learning the ropes wasn't easy and, in many instances, I didn't feel Ned's outlook was necessarily in accord with my Christian viewpoint. Maybe that was my first mistake. Ned was matter-of-fact and pragmatic and didn't look *too* closely at the merits of a case. If a bloke was in trouble and on a disciplinary charge then Ned automatically assumed that his chief function was to get the gaffer off the man's back. At first, I regarded this attitude as completely immoral, but I soon learned to put my blinkers on and ignore the finer points of morality. There was a tacit understanding on the part of men and management that morality was a big word with elastic sides.

At first I would listen to all the complaints that came my way and take a sympathetic view, but Ned soon put me right.

'Listen to all their bellyaching and nod your head in the right places, but remember – you can't afford to go into the gaffer's office with every gripe the blokes cough up. There are some areas of negotiation which only *we* know about and it wouldn't be in the best interests of the blokes to let 'em know *everything*. It'd only put 'em on hosses they couldn't ride. Another thing, these blokes don't *always* tell you the whole story; they only tell you that bit that suits their case. So, agree with them and then go into a quiet corner and chew the cud.'

During the next three years I chewed the cud till it curdled and went sour.

One of the best, albeit cynical, definitions of a leader is that he is a man who hears a crowd marching down the street, places himself at the head of the column and shouts, 'Follow me!' This description rather fitted my role as a leader because at the time of my election to the shop steward's office, amenity reorganization in the factory was well under way, and in the shed where I worked renewal of the men's washing facilities commenced. The general impression was that I had something to do about the speedy implementation of the plans. Usually, any progress in this field moved at the speed of cold tar so I basked in the afterglow of the men's congratulations. The truth was that the new wash basins and drinking fountains were a complete surprise to me. But my reputation as 'the bloke that gets things done' enormously bolstered my ego.

The gaffer's office was alongside the amenity block, and he kept a north eye for any man washing his hands before the specified time. Indeed, his office was seventy-five per cent glass construction so that he had a clear view of all that was taking place in the stores. Any larking about or blatant disregard of the rules would be instantly noted and acted upon; his eyrie was also strategically sited to watch the clocking machine. This was an area constantly under his eagle eye. Of course, the men could also see what was taking place in his office and when the shop stewards were in discussion they assessed loss or gain, victory or defeat, by how much desk-bashing the boss did and vice-versa. A good old grand slam with threats and counter-threats would provide plenty of fuel for discussion around the sacred fane – the mashing can – during the ten minute break in the morning.

More importantly, these discussions in the gaffer's office would be validated by concrete results favouring the men's point of view. If the conversation was about gardening or Monty Python and there was general bonhomie with smiles all round – as sometimes happened – then the men would regard this with the greatest suspicion. Although they could not hear what was taking place, they gauged that mutual goodwill was a bad omen for the future. I noted this and observed that bosses and men's representatives should recognize certain lines of social demarcation – if the gaffer grins in your presence, keep a straight face and explain to the blokes he was suffering from indigestion.

My Christian witness began to pall a little. I felt I had to compromise in my personal relationships. Hitherto I had regarded the chief foreman as a decent chap doing a thankless job. True, at times he was stubborn and impatient, but I had categorized him as 'not one of the best but better than the worst.' I realized that if I was to maintain my standing with the men, with the degree of confidence necessary to enable me to carry out my duties as their elected representative, then I had to adopt a role and fit into a well-defined category.

My colleagues on the Works and Shops Committee had

no such inhibitions. There was a clear demarcation in their minds. Their loyalties lay in the working class movement and the implementation of Socialist policies. I had no strong political leanings. So, at the outset of my three year stint as a shop steward, I felt I was out on a limb and I experienced a sense of isolation in my relationship with the rest of the Shop Stewards' Committee. This was brought sharply into focus when British Rail, in collaboration with the trades union and with the blessing of both Government and Opposition, introduced the closed shop policy. I felt this to be a clear violation of workers' rights and a sinister erosion of personal liberty.

I approached Sam Stodd and explained my doubts. 'I've a problem,' I began. 'I've no political axe to grind, and, as you probably know, Sam, I objected to paying the political levy, so what I have to say has no political bias.'

Sam sympathetically nodded his head and I followed him into his office and we sat down.

'Smoke?' he offered, pulling out his cigarettes. 'No thanks, Sam. As you know, I'm a bread and butter steward; I can't get hot under the collar about union affairs, but I am bothered about the implementation of the closed shop'.

Sam looked at me and smiled a slow gentle smile, and then he shook his head sadly as one might do to an erring son.

'Ralph! Ralph!' he said. 'Can you practice medicine without belonging to the BMA? Or be a lawyer without being a member of the Law Society?'

'I don't suppose so,' I replied, rather unsure of my ground.

'There!' he said triumphantly. 'These professional guys have their unions and closed shops but they call 'em by fancy names.'

'But what about personal freedom? How about some bloke who has scruples – religious, moral grounds for not belonging to a union?'

'OK. What about your moral obligations to your mates who finance highly competent officials to negotiate your wages and conditions – people who act on your behalf? How about legal representation if you have to fight an industrial injury? What about widows' rights if you get killed at work? Surely you don't expect in a nationalized industry this size – some 250,000 people – that each man can negotiate his own rises. Come off it Ralph!'

So I came off it and later, when twenty-odd men were sacked for not joining the union I felt like Judas.

There were other areas where I felt a sense of alienation from my colleagues on the Shop Stewards' Committee. The Social Club for example. When the year's leisure activities were being discussed there were a number of suggestions. 'A one-day trip to Scarborough, with sea fishing.' 'A local fishing match.' 'A buffet and dance at the Welfare Club.' 'A strip-show.' 'A trip to an away football match.' 'A trip to York – with fishing.'

As will be noted, the piscatorial art figured large in the expectations of the Shop Stewards' Committee. None of the proposed activities particularly appealed to me. I was not going to suggest my particular bent – a trip to Malvern Priory in order to inspect the misericords. The idea of trying to socialize with my mates was about as inspiring as studying the Wigan telephone directory. So be it . . .

Again, there were startled gasps when the sacred cow of overtime was raised and I advanced my point of view. The Labour Movement, having fought for the forty-hour working week and at that time currently pursuing the thirty-five hour working week, was being systematically sabotaged by men and management alike by their common desire to incorporate overtime in their bargaining procedures. As an inducement, the carrot of overtime was dangled before the men not simply to increase output but as a means of increasing the size of the wage packet; overtime became a bargaining factor in its own right.

I once had a man visit me who wanted to see the Works

welfare officer 'because banning my overtime is causing me nervous tension'. The man in question had a Monday–Tuesday syndrome: far too frequently he was absent from work on these days because of 'backache' (a well-known symptom the doctor finds great difficulty in diagnosing). Consequently, the management – quite rightly – banned him from making up his lost days by working overtime at increased rates of pay. In this case, overtime was an artificial stimulus to a higher wage packet. But the system worked both ways. The gaffer could justify his presence at work on Sunday because the men were also working on their rest day, and of course, *his* rate of pay was considerably higher than the men's. The 'bite at the cherry' as it was euphemistically called might in other circumstances be called a capitalistic trick to kid the British worker that he was well-off, no matter how many hours he had slogged away at work. Certainly, the witholding of overtime from a man was considered to be a salutary punishment. On some jobs – maintenance for example – overtime was absolutely necessary, but in very many cases it was an expensive way of keeping up morale on the shop floor.

2

The Rulebook

I decided first of all to get acquainted with the British Rail rulebook, the manual which covers all aspects of railway operations. Most of the contents of this book are irrelevant to the workshop staff but on reflection, it is easy to see how simple it would be to bring the system to a halt by meticulous observance of the rules . . . 'Before taking charge (of the train) the driver must satisfy himself that the traction unit is in order, making sure the loco has two sets of track operating clips and a sealed case containing twelve detonators and two red flags. . . the guard must have a whistle and a watch which is showing the correct time and must take with him on the train a handlamp, a red and green flag, not less than twelve detonators and such other articles . . .' and so on.

The rulebook, so far as I was concerned, related to matters like discipline and situations in which a man might get the sack, or be suspended without pay. In discussions I had with Ned I was assured that much of my time would be spent in acting as advocate on Form One charges – the disciplinary procedure laid down.

An employee is 'expected to be prompt, civil and obliging to the public, dressed tidily and he must not drink on duty, solicit gratuities or use his transistor except in places specifically authorized'. In short, the Archangel Gabriel would just about fit the role of a model BR employee. Ned, with his dirty boots, two-day growth, donkey jacket, egg-flecked jersey, greasy courduroys that could remain vertical without his legs being in them, and with a clapped out transistor in his pocket that could only get medium wave, would certainly not be the kind of employee the architects of the rulebook had in mind. But we were all familiar with the rules and the bosses winked at the mild transgressions of the men. That is, until it suited their purpose to 'make an example' and tighten up on slack discipline.

Standing on the clock waiting to knock off at 12:21 is a punishable offence, but not at 12:22 – that's OK. Occasionally, in order to create an efficient atmosphere and improve general discipline, the rules are enforced, and Sam Sludge is on the carpet for being on the clock four minutes before time. It's hard for Sam to realize that if 4,000 men waste two minutes of the gaffers' time that represents 133 working hours lost.

Under the Work Study arrangement every man has six minutes RA (Relaxation Allowance) built into his working day. Smoking, reading, the call of nature – all these activities are provided for in the six minutes RA. Diarrhoea and dyslexia aren't taken into account.

The maincrop of the shop steward's problems come precisely in the area where there is tension between personal liberty and authority. One of my first 'cases' involved Wayne, a gangling youth with a deceptively sanguine outlook on life. Wayne was a fork-lift truck driver and he came to me one day with a problem. He had been given a disciplinary letter charging him with being asleep on duty in the cab of his lift truck. Wayne protested vehemently to me that he 'wasn't flamin' well sleeping'. Apparently, the day had been hot and the air in the tiny cabin of his vehicle was heavy and humid. Wayne went on to describe what had happened.

'I'd just taken a load of buffers to the shop and was waiting for the next job. I propped my feet on the steering wheel and leaned back an' just closed my eyes . . .'

'You were dozing?'

'I wasn't dozing,' he replied irately, 'I was just thinkin'.'

'About the next job?'

'Yes, that's it – the next job, I was thinkin' of the next job!'

'What happened then?'

'Well, my back was sort of arched against the door and, suddenly, I felt the door give way an' my flamin' 'ead nearly fell off as I fell out. I looked up an' there was this gaffer 'n 'is mate, the under-foreman. "Oh," 'e said, "copped you. You was sleepin'." "Don't be flamin' daft," I replied. "I wasn't sleepin', I was thinkin'".'

'Thinking', I said quizzically, 'with your eyes closed and your feet propped on the steering wheel?'

''onest Ralph, I was thinkin' about the next job.'

'Then what happened?'

'Next thing, this gaffer looked at me 'n said, "You're due for a Form One," and Wayne handed me the buff coloured disciplinary note spelling out the charge and inviting him to state his defence either in writing or at a personal interview accompanied by an advocate – a fellow employee or his shop steward.

'Fill it in, tell 'em you want a personal interview, and bung it back in the office,' I advised. 'Tell them you weren't sleeping, just thinking with your eyes shut, and put me down as your spokesman.' Wayne went away somewhat reassured and I echoed Anatole France's words that 'he who gives hope gives everything'. There is a certain consolation in having an accredited representative of the union around when management decides to bring out the big stick.

The foreman in question approached me later in the week and invited my comments. 'I've had Wayne's form back concerning that incident the other day and I see he's nominated you to speak on his behalf. Surely you don't think he can bleedin' well get away with *sleeping* on duty?'

'I'm not saying he was sleeping and I'm not saying he wasn't. Just wait and see. I'll see you in your office when you find it convenient to have an interview,' I replied diplomatically.

During the next few days this gaffer suffered from verbal diarrhoea and was heard to remark that he'd 'make Wayne stew'. But Wayne didn't stew. Wayne was hard gristle.

Indeed, when the day of the interview was announced Wayne decided to take the day appointed as a voluntary 'holiday' and went sick. The gaffer was not impressed when Wayne showed his face next day; we were informed the hearing was to take place within the hour.

Wayne swore and threatened dire action so I cautioned him, 'Shurrup Wayne, that won't help. Just keep your mouth shut and answer Yes or No. Don't start arguing. Leave it to me!'

We were called into the office and the gaffer's spiel was well rehearsed. 'I don't like disciplining my men. We are part of a team and must all pull together . . . I don't like these confrontations but I've got a job to do . . .'

Wayne looked into the nebulous reaches of the oak plaque stuck on the wall behind the gaffer's head inscribed with the deathless words: 1935 Annual Show. First Prize in Kidney Bean Section: Ernest Guffton. Supplies Department.

'Have you anything to say?' enquired the gaffer in a not unkindly tone.

Wayne jerked his head in my direction and said, 'Yeh, we want proof I was asleep.'

'Proof? What *proof*?'

'Just . . . proof!

'What he means is, what evidence have you got that Wayne was actually asleep,' I explained.

'Me and the gaffer from twelve Shop *saw* him!'

'You'd better put out a mayday call and fetch him to substantiate that statement, otherwise we shall be forced to bring in the Works Committee!' I replied.

The Works Committee represented the next stage in the machinery and that body was the strongest line of defence – the Big Brother, solidly behind the worker. In any case, the gaffer would not relish the idea of the matter being escalated to that level. There was an uneasy silence as he pressed a buzzer and despatched a runner to bring in his witness from twelve Shop. We stood there and felt his eyes snarling in our direction. Presently, the other gaffer arrived, smart and smug, thirty-ish and opportunity-knocked.

'Did you or did you not cop Wayne Goodhall here asleep in his cab on the 16th?'

'Certainly, we *both* copped him!'

'OK,' I said, 'now *prove* he was asleep.'

'We *saw* him.'

'Did you hear him snoring?'

'Don't be daft!'

'He wasn't snoring. You didn't cop him sleepwalking – he'd just got his eyes shut with his feet propped on the steering wheel and he'd only just switched the engine off – don't *you* be daft. This charge won't stick if we take it higher.'

'But he nearly fell out of his cab when we opened the door!' exploded the first gaffer.

'If I kicked your chair from under you *you'd* cock over.'

With an impatient wave of his hand the foreman signified the interview was over. 'I'll let you know my verdict,' he said testily.

A few days later Wayne was handed a letter saying he was to be awarded one day's suspension and loss of pay which, to Wayne with three kids and a council rent was stiff.

'I've got a good mind to tell him to stuff his job,' glowered Wayne.

'Well don't. We'll appeal.'

The appeal eventually went to the big boss in the top office and he took a somewhat different view of the circumstances of the case. After a very severe verbal warning, Wayne got off the charge and a few days later, the gaffer who preferred the charge against Wayne, delivered the *coup de grâce*. He looked at me with the air of a man who had just had a revelation and said, 'Ralph, I don't know how you can call yourself a Christian and be a shop steward.'

Later that evening I sat by the fire and talked things over with Pat, my wife.

'But the Church is always advocating more Christians ought to be involved at shop floor level,' she said.

'I know, but the people that advocate involvement are generally academics who see things in straight lines. If that bloke was asleep – and I think he was – and I had said so in the gaffer's office, I wouldn't have lasted another day as shop steward. The blokes would have taken a vote of no confidence. It was my job to get him off. I was his *advocate*. Well, I got him off and had to bend my conscience in the process.'

'Do you think it might be better to give up before you get too involved? I mean, to do the job properly surely you're supposed to go to branch meetings and suchlike?'

'That's true but there are a good many shop stewards who never bother to go to a branch meeting unless there's a dispute fizzing in the barrel, and it's a well-known fact that the rank and file never turn up. They're just apathetic.'

'But aren't *you* apathetic?'

'I suppose I am. But there again, I've got plenty to do at church.'

Pat, who recognized the truth of that last statement, snuffed out our conversation with the usual night time formula: 'Oh well, I'll make a cup of Ovaltine and we'll pray about it.'

Throughout my period of office I was troubled by the difficulty of reconciling my Christian standing with the role expected of me. I felt vulnerable to the tensions and pressures. Sometimes I was forced to adopt a kind of industrial 'situational ethic' when what seemed to me to be the right course of action, activated by a sense of love and brotherly kindness, conflicted with authority. I could quite understand the difficulty of a Christian who was a member of a heavy labouring gang, working alongside his mates unloading a wagon. When the gang knocked off for a smoke or to listen to the latest score in a football match did he look pious and carry on working, or did he fall in with the rest and 'twist' his employer? Did he walk away when dirty jokes were being cracked, or stay and look uncomfortable and embarrassed? I quickly recognized how a Christian shop steward is doubly vulnerable. He must be true to his Christian conviction while at the same time seeing the problems on the shop floor in their particular context.

Maybe Jacques Ellul was right when he observed that the danger as far as the Church is concerned is of seeing the world's problems as the world sees them. Having a Christian perspective on moral values is one thing, but when it comes to implementing those principles at grass-roots level it becomes quite another. The safe way is to swing up the drawbridge, maintain our defences and, in splendid isolation, sling in a few Gospel shots from the battlements. But that is an odd way to fight a war. And, indeed, when Christ spoke of the Church he referred to it in terms of an attacking force (Matt. 16.18).

One is forced to conclude that when Christianity puts on its heavy working boots and tramps into the dirty harvest field, some of the muck sticks. The charge levelled against Christ was that he sought company with sinners. Indeed, his whole life was a series of calculated risks. Loving the world as he loved it, yielding up our lives as he yielded up his, bearing the brandmarks of the cross as he bore them involves a high degree of involvement with society *as it is* and this includes the possibility of getting dirty. In practical terms it will often mean conflict with accepted practices and codes of conduct. The gaffer who pinches a pen, parks on a double line, fiddles his income tax return; the employee who clocks his mate's card, repairs his punctured inner tube in the Works time, plays his transistor at the bench – there are so many muddy furrows in the harvest field. Ballpoint pens, buff-coloured forms, clock cards, private transport, transistor radios all have necessitated some form of legislation, and the lines of Christian morality are becoming more extended, more blurred, more complex and indistinct. In a society so integrated as ours the old Marxist conception of Them and Us no longer applies. But, in the light of Inland Revenue, radar traps, census returns and so on, we may conclude that the whole nameless, faceless amorphous Establishment that controls our lives is the Them. Maybe Max Weber, the renowned father of modern sociology, was right when he declared that the growth of bureaucracy, and not the class struggle, is the key factor in the modern world.

Having taken up the challenge of representing my fellow workers I was heavily committed to a sectional view of life and automatically regarded by management and men as fulfilling a defined role. I was expected to fit into the mould; any departure would have been looked upon as, at the least a nuisance to be tolerated, and at the most, a threat to be quietly suffocated.

3

Safety First

When I first entered a rail workshop – in 1947 – it was an unnerving experience. In the forge, for example, angry furnaces belched out acrid fumes and in spite of the ventilation equipment and extraction fans, a blue, choking haze hung on the air. Behind strong metal shields, sweating men expertly probed the blinding heart of the furnaces with long steel pincers and with deceptive ease, tossed metal strips to their mates. They in turn placed the white-hot metal onto anvils and methodically, with great skill, the metal was beaten into shape.

Alleyways were paved with steel slabs and straddled with tiers of glowing red springs and ironwork of all kinds. Everywhere there was dust and seeming chaos as overhead, travelling cranes noisily clanked along steel runners lifting bars of metal to other bays. The workshop, to the uninitiated, was a fearful place for one felt that in whatever direction one moved there was an imminent danger of being impaled, crushed, burned alive, asphyxiated, or simply dropping dead through sheer fright. But working conditions have vastly improved over the last few years. Barrier cream to protect the skin, sound proofing of noisy machines, safety glasses, free towels, industrial gloves – the accent is now very much on safety and healthy working conditions; even so, the shop floor can be a potentially dangerous place.

Let us suppose it is an average working day and four fictional characters – Jack, Bob, John and Steve set off for work. Their wives have packed the sandwiches and filled their tea flasks. They call at the newsagents for the *Mirrors* and *Suns* and buy their packets of fags. They clock in and start the morning shift, but before the end of the working day they will be dead through industrial accidents; their wives will be widows; their children fatherless. Or maybe Jack, Bob, John and Steve form part of the thousands who are injured every day at work — injuries which necessitate three or more days off work.

Your hard-pressed executive might suffer an occupational hazard such as a coronary but the factory worker is exposed to a much wider variety of physical dangers associated with his job. Air pollution, dangers to the skin, inadequately guarded machines, welding dangers, fire, noise-hazards; in a large engineering works the Safety Committee is of vital importance in reducing those awful statistics of death and injury. An accident at work ceases to be a mere statistic when it happens to a mate. I recall the tragedy a few years ago when a crane suddenly swivelled and took off a man's head; and the time when a high wind caught a sheet of thin gauge metal and neatly sliced a man's arm. Then there was the inexpertly handled fork-lift truck which crushed a man's foot and the carboy of acid that tilted the wrong way and made a very nasty mess of a man's arm. I was once called to an incident where a buffer, hydraulically compressed, suddenly exploded as it was being unloaded from a rail wagon. The labourer who was handling it narrowly escaped serious injury to his face as he collapsed backwards and away from the source of the explosion.

Ned and me, as shop representatives, were members of the Safety Committee and a good deal of useful work was accomplished by this very important body.

My mate, Ernie, worked in the sawmill and after thirty-five years in that place, it was perfectly understandable that every month or so he took a couple of days off work. Ernie was working in an atmosphere of high-pitched whistles and metallic screeching; the exposure limit of ninety decibels was constantly being exceeded. Consequently, his eight-hour working day was spent standing by his planing machine wearing ear-protectors. When Ernie was home, he shouted and his wife understandably took no notice, although strangers might have thought he was always in a bad mood.

Exposure to excessive noise accelerates normal loss of hearing, as Ernie discovered to his cost. But while he had any sense of hearing, he left the sawmill each day with screeching in his ears. The 'Sabbath rest by Galilee' and 'calm of hills above' was a world removed from Ernie's place of work. A saying in the Works was that you could always tell whether a man had worked in the sawmill — if he had he would be minus a finger or a thumb. The saying bears testimony to the fact that even the basic safety regulations were not always regarded with the diligence which might reduce those daily casualty figures.

Even today, shoulder length hair, for example, might be fashionable for the young apprentices, but after it has been wound round an automatic high-speed lathe neither the hair or the scalp looks pretty; hair nets catch on very quickly after an accident.

When I first started on the railways as a labourer I worked alongside a character named Willie. He was a pathetic chap with a speech impediment caused by an accident during the war. It seems he got in the way of a recoil from a twenty-five-pounder gun and sustained terrible facial disfigurement and a permanent injury to the roof of his mouth. At the time he was engaged to be married but tragically, his bride-to-be could not cope with the strange character who came home on sick-leave from a military hospital and she threw him over. Poor Willie blew a mental fuse and spent a long time in a psychiatric hospital. When he was eventually discharged he was not altogether 'normal' but he did manage to get a job on the railway where he spent his time in the workshops swilling out the pits under the lathes where the evil-smelling cutting oil — the coolant which kept the temperature down on the metal being worked — drained off.

'Silly Willie' as the men called him would pick hot

pennies off the shop floor with his teeth for a laugh. He would also be the butt for all kinds of good-natured, and often cruel, practical jokes. Moreover, Willie smelt of cutting oil. His clothes were rotten and saturated with the stuff. Neither he or his sister, with whom he lived, seemed unduly concerned about the matter. His skin was permanently in contact with the irritant and there was an angry red rash covering his body. Eventually, he knocked off work and it came as no surprise to learn that he was sick. His sickness did not last very long; in a very few weeks he was dead and his death was attributed to one of those obscure complaints that have a blanket word to cover the lot. Rumour had it that Willie died of cancer of the scrotum. What we didn't realize at the time was the danger to which Willie was exposed as he leaned over his barrow in his saturated overalls . . .

It is only since 1960 that serious steps have been taken to deal with the cancer-forming agents in the coolant oils used in industry. A worker whose job entails straddling a machine where this type of oil is used is prone to cancer of the scrotum unless particular care is taken to ensure absolute cleanliness. For example, his overalls *must* be dry-cleaned; wet-washing removes only fifty per cent of oil contamination. The frightening thing is that, like asbestosis, the effect of contamination may be hidden for thirty years or more.

When we open the newspaper and read of 'wildcat strikes', 'kangaroo courts' and 'militant unionism' it is as well to remember that there is a vast amount of useful and necessary work undertaken by the unpaid shop steward in this particular field of health and safety at work. If he does his homework conscientiously, the shop representative will take note of the bewildering variety of gases, fumes and vapours that are daily released into the working environment.

To see some men performing their duties in the works is an education in sartorial discrimination. Protective clothing includes goggles, safety footwear, aprons, loose-fitting gloves, ear-protectors, helmets, hoods, respirators . . . In fact, all the equipment necessary to deal with anything from acetone to jaw-cracking components like polytetrafluoro-ethylene (PTFE).

Monitoring the number of workers suffering from chest, stomach or eye troubles in a given work-area is often an indication that the TLVs (Threshold Limit Values) – the maximum amount of pollution substances allowed into the working atmosphere – have been breached. It is an interesting fact that over five hundred substances have been given TLVs. But TLV limits are only used by the factory inspectorate as a guide; they still have no legal force.

Then there are the unknown hazards connected with some jobs. Medical opinion is divided on the long-term effects of, for example, welding fumes. Some experts claim they are not a long-term serious danger to health, but other doctors are not so sure. Short-term effects of breathing in toxic welding fumes vary from minor throat irritation, catarrh or a slight cough, to metal-fume fever. Coupled with the X-ray and gamma-ray equipment used to radio-graphically inspect welds and the noise level in excess of ninety decibels in certain specialized types of welding, the welders job, whilst highly-paid, isn't the safest of occupations.

From a Christian perspective I realized that I was my brother's keeper in this matter of health and safety on the shop floor, and I was forced to conclude that in the long-term we must pay a high price for our technological prowess.

A death actually occuring during the course of a man doing his job is a nine-day wonder. Some years ago, the old goods department building in Back Street was one of the first casualties to fall under the Beeching axe. The whole area was scheduled for redevelopment and a gang of rail-men had been sent to clear the area. At the same time, the

23

demolition contractors were at work on the site. I recall it was a hot July Saturday afternoon. The sun scorched the melting asphalt and in retrospect I suppose the torpid heat was a contributory factor to the blokes relaxing their vigilance regarding normal safety procedure.

I was on my way to change my library books and was passing near to Back Street when I heard a low rumble like thunder. I paused for a moment, wondering what it might be and seconds later heard the banshee wail of a fire engine followed by other ominous sirens. A small knot of people had congregated at the top of Back Street and I joined them. Apparently, a ten-foot wall had collapsed, burying one of the railmen. Within minutes squads of police, ambulancemen and firemen were standing on the heap of rubble using scaffolding as improvised crowbars to prise away large pieces of the wall. Some of the railmen were working alongside, clawing ferociously with their bare hands and throwing bricks aside. A man from the crowd walked up to the fire chief and offered to drive a dumper-truck and push some of the rubble aside and his offer was gratefully accepted. The 'official' driver was vomiting in a corner – he had caused the tragedy by backing into the partially demolished wall. The crowd stood mute and only the harsh sound of metal on stone could be heard as the rescuers toiled away.

A woman clutching her shopping bag in one hand and a small child in the other looked on. The child's piping voice kept asking: 'What are they doing, mum?' Two nurses stood by, with the ambulance doors open and a stretcher ready.

Suddenly, there was an unearthly squeal – almost like a wounded animal – and the crowd gave a low moan. Sweating police and firemen worked with a new urgency. Then, at a signal from one of the police officers, the ambulancemen clambered up on to the rubble with a stretcher as a large piece of masonry was levered gently off the still form beneath. The man's face was just recognizable. His arm slipped lifelessly off his chest as they laid him on the stretcher.

Somebody in the crowd tapped a policeman on the shoulder. 'Your trousers, mate,' he said helpfully, 'there's blood on your trouser leg'. With a murmured 'Thanks,' the police officer wiped off a jellied piece of red tissue.

The excitement was over and the sombre crowd slowly drifted away. On the following Monday morning there was the usual post-mortem over the teabreak.

'Why does God allow things like *that*?' I was asked.

'I don't know', I replied. 'I don't suppose the wisest man in the whole world knows the answer to that question.'

'It's immoral,' my questioner retorted.

'I guess it's the price we pay for being what we are,' I said.

He turned to his companions, 'Fancy Arsenal making a draw on Saturday . . .'

On the spot where the tragedy occurred there is now a supermarket and in my head, a statistic became something infinitely more important than a mere cipher . . .

4

The Computer Cometh

When British Rail decided to radically change their system of stores operations they did it unilaterally, and without reference to the men on the shop floor. The introduction of a computerized system was an innovation none of us were prepared for. Data Capture machines were to replace the manual method of receiving, storing and issuing material and this was to be inflicted on the men without prior consultation.

We felt aggrieved, to put it mildly, and the men were vociferous in putting their feelings to the management through their shop stewards. Ned and me were absolutely at one in our determination not to be bulldozed into the technological future of operating the supplies department. In our judgement, pressing buttons and using computer jargon was a world removed from the traditional picture of the store-bloke. He was a flat-capped character with a muffler round his neck armed with a stubby pencil and a fag behind his ear, and he'd usually write down snap bits of information on the back of his empty fag packet.

'How much do you think it's worth to press the buttons?' asked Ned.

'Three quid at least,' I replied.

'We'll ask for five quid in that case,' said Ned, his chin jutting out more firmly.

So, having heard through the grape vine that we would shortly be asked to go into the office when the question of introducing the machines would be formally put to us, we decided to adopt the time-honoured policy of witholding co-operation until some agreement on payment for operating the machines was concluded. The men unanimously agreed that five quid was a reasonable price but of course, we knew, and management knew, that the figure was completely unrealistic.

'If we goin' to wear white coats and ponce about with little buttons like the tarts in the office, they ought to flamin' well pay us staff-status!'

'I'm fifty. Do they just think they can alter a man's cussin' working style without consulting him?'

'They can stuff the machines. If the gaffers say, "It's a good thing", there's summat wrong somewhere.'

'How many blokes will get the sack through redundancy by these machines being introduced?'

'What's the saving to British Rail and what do we get out of it?'

'We'll be gormless zombies after two bleedin' hours pushing them buttons!'

And so on.

I agreed with many of the men's comments. In retrospect, resistance to change was utterly predictable and it was difficult to see how the question of computerization could have been introduced without meeting resistance. Maybe the question should have been raised by our full-time union representatives who might have been more sensitive to shop floor feeling on the matter. In any case, it did seem an imposition on the part of management to suddenly try to alter traditional working methods. Many felt it was totally inhuman.

There was the classic case of old Jack who was doing his best to keep abreast of the speed-up in production – without the computer – and under 'normal' working conditions. All his working life had been spent in British Rail workshops and his bolt store had, at one time, been a model of efficiency. Of late however, Jack had become a little doddery and forgetful. His domestic life was turned upside down because his wife spent extended periods in a mental hospital suffering from acute depression. Jack had

27

to start work all over again after finishing his day shift in the factory. His wife was incapable of doing the domestic chores and when she was away in hospital, Jack looked after himself and visited her diligently.

But the hard face of British industry took little account of Jack's plight. True, there were sympathetic murmurings but the question of Jack making mistakes and falling down on his job began to be orchestrated by quiet threats to discipline him. Needless to say, we monitored these snarls from management, feeling that if it came to the crunch we might have to take some form of action ourselves.

Jack's problem seemed to mirror the dilemma facing many in British industry today. The old time craftsmen, the men who took hold of English timber and with rare skill fashioned the Pullman coaches that were once the envy of the world, are no more. Prefabricated metal and plastics have effectively made their skills expensive and redundant.

Poor old Jack could not cope with the computer and in due course, after consultation between his shop stewards and the management, he was quietly transferred to a less demanding job and trouble was avoided.

Ned and me called a general meeting of the men at which we outlined the proposals of the management to introduce the new system. The overall feeling at the end of the meeting was that if there was no money at the end of the line then the whole idea was a dead duck.

We conveyed this unanimous view to the bosses and they immediately countered by informing us that no *definite* arrangements to place the machines in the supplies department had been made; that planning was in the formative stages; that in any case, a period of training to operate the machines would have to take place. In short, management was saying, 'Don't overreact; don't jump the gun!'

The negotiating procedure had run true to form at this stage. The Eastern bazaar system of bargaining was being

28

pursued. A period of stalemate followed when both sides, after the initial sally, decided to retire and allow a larger perspective to develop . . . until one April morning.

Ned came to me in high dudgeon. 'Hey up, Ralph, they've brought six of the flamin' machines into the Main Stores.'

'What flamin' machines?' I asked innocently.

'The flamin' tin boxes full of wires!' howled Ned.

So, we went to view the 'tin boxes full of wires'. They stood, all chrome and plastic, shining with white buttons and a console like an expensive hi-fi with twin speakers.

'They ain't bein' installed!' said Ned flatly.

'We can't stop them being installed,' I said, 'but we can stop the blokes from pushing the buttons.'

'The blokes won't *want* to push the buttons,' murmured Ned.

A few days later when the dust was beginning to settle on the machines we were called into the office and told that if we so desired, we could go to another depot in the north of England and actually *see* the new system being operated. This was a revelation to us. We had no idea that any good trade unionist would be so daft as to operate the machines without adequate remuneration and this, we understood, was not the case at the depot we had been invited to visit. We retired to consult with Sam Stodd and George Grundy. They were most emphatic.

'You must both go, and we'll also send two representatives of the Committee,' they told us.

So, we accepted the management's offer, subject to allowing two members of the Works Committee (the inner core of the negotiating machinery within the Works) to accompanying us as 'onlookers'. This condition was readily accepted and with an embargo on the machines still in force, Ned and me, together with Joe and Steve from the Committee, boarded a train for the north.

On the journey we exchanged views on politics and life in general. Both Joe and Steve were knowledgeable blokes.

Steve particularly was an erudite character and being widely read, quoted easily from the classics. His Maoist philosophy was well-grounded and he presented a very cogent view of the way Western capitalism was lurching to an inevitable close. Surprisingly, he had a sympathetic view of the Church and was open to discuss the deeper implication of his views. Somewhat wistfully he confessed he 'wished he had faith to believe' and was willing to talk to knowledgeable people in the local church at some future date about politics and Christianity. Here I felt was a genuine seeker after truth. Indeed, he said he 'had a homin' instinct to believe in Somebody out there'. He readily accepted that his Maoist philosophy was only a credible alternative to something deeper.

When we arrived at the depot we received the treatment usually accorded VIPs. A car was provided to whisk us to the point of our enquiry and we chatted chummily to the member of the management staff who was acting as our chauffeur and guide. He had obviously been tipped off to give us the old pals treatment. According to him, the new system was operating very successfully and was far superior to the old method of storekeeping.

'Who says so?' asked Steve, laconically, as we were driven along.

His Nibs kept his eyes firmly on the road in front as he replied, 'From everyone's point of view, I should say it's a better way of conducting our business.' The character was a born diplomat and hand-picked for the delicate task of softening us up.

'How much extra are your blokes being paid?' Ned asked.

The wintry smile on the boss's face evaporated and the atmosphere became decidedly arctic. 'I think it would be better if you had a look at the situation before replying to that question' he replied, a little spiky.

We pulled up in the Works and he looked at his watch. 'Look chaps,' he said, 'the lads knock off for their midday break in fifteen minutes. We have the Works canteen, or there's a nice little pub down the road – it's up to you where you want to go'.

Steve and Joe opted for the pub while Ned and myself went to the canteen. We arranged to meet again at one-thirty.

The Works canteen had the same greasy smell as the one back home, and the tables were covered with yellowing plastic. A crocodile of men in blue dungarees chatted like budgies against a background of piped music. The long line filed past a bevy of jolly ladies who exchanged saucy pleasantries as they served the pie and chips. We had spent most of the day in reaching our venue, and time was pressing heavily, so after sampling the weak tea, and eating our sandwiches, we took leave of the depressing atmosphere – the piped music, plastic tables and green walls – and made our way back to the prearranged meeting place.

Steve and Joe smelt like Strong's Brewery and their reflexes were not as sharp as they might have been so we decided to split up. They went with 'Himmler' – the sobriquet Ned had conferred on our managerial guide – and we wandered off on our own. But first, we were formally introduced to the men who were operating the new machines. Understandably, with the boss around the men were reluctant to say too much, but when we spoke to them out of range of the gaffer's ear they were very vocal.

'No leadership,' said their unofficial spokesman. 'We haven't got stewards of the right calibre. The management just moved the things in one day and boom! boom! – that was it!'

'There ought to have been a national agreement regarding payment,' said another.

'Biggest bleedin' box-up since Dunkirk.'

'Made some of the blokes sick . . .'

There was a good deal of mistrust regarding the motives of the management in introducing the system without prior consultation at local level. The men were understandably apprehensive about the future. If such a revolutionary alteration in the working methods could be introduced almost overnight, what other technological beasts might softly pad out of the top office?

I came to the conclusion that while the machines were simple to operate, they performed functions which had previously been undertaken by the clerks in the office. Again, it seemed the critical processing of data which was previously spread over a number of people at various stages in the clerical chain were now concentrated on the man who operated the machine, and this concentration of responsibility ought to be adequately rewarded.

After our quick tour of the Works we held a postmortem. I asked Himmler how many clerks had been made redundant by the machine. The question came in at a rather oblique angle and caught him unaware.

'Oh, about fifteen I should think – but!' he added hastily, 'natural wastage, absorption into other departments – nobody sacked you understand!'

We understood alright and the journey back home was spent in assessing our chances of securing a reasonable price for the job. Steve and Joe with more experience in these matters thought there was only a marginal possibility, bearing in mind the Government's pay policy, but Ned spoke for both of us when he pointed out that 'only a fool would take on more responsibility for the same money'. We decided to play it cool and wait for management to take the initiative.

It may have been coincidence, or the sharp point of a guilty conscience, or maybe a heightened sensitivity to basic Christian precepts, but it seemed over the next few weeks almost every sermon in church included a word on 'giving more than getting'; on self-control; on the readiness of the Christian to bend low in recognition of the Lordship of Christ. Hearing this at church on Sunday was fine but when it came to Monday morning and the steady stream of comments from my mates about the iniquitous system of British Rail's future planning, I felt wobbly in my Christian walk. On the one hand I was saying 'Amen' to the preacher, but on the other, I was advocating industrial action if our demands were not met.

The action I proposed was a policy of non-co-operation which would effectively snarl up the works. I suggested to the men that while we had no power to stop the machines being installed, nor yet an official mandate from our union to spike a training programme drawn up by the management, we could effectively stop full implementation of the project. The feeling of the men was that this was the policy to adopt and a letter to this effect was sent to the management.

Softly, softly, catchee monkee . . . the next step was the siting of the machines on the factory floor and an intimation that a training schedule had been drawn up for 'selected personnel'. The two shop representatives were to be in the first intake in order to monitor the system.

Ned and me reported on the first training session to the instructor, a southerner with a po-faced outlook on life. He gave me the impression that he had lived that long with the computer he couldn't live without it. In a flat monotone he recited how the thing worked, what it did, what it couldn't do and the monologue gradually took on a different meaning: he began referring to the machine as *he*. '*He* will refuse to accept this', '*he* will reject that', '*he* will function the material', and so on. In paternal phrases the po-faced young man from Hemel Hempstead pounded to the finishing post, leaving us all wondering.

'Any questions?' he asked in a tone of voice which suggested a tired expectancy of catalogued enquiries.

'How much are we being paid extra for usin' the flamin' thing?' was the first daft question from one of our number. He was sharply told to shut up by Ned and then the questions came thick and fast.

There was no doubt the instructor had done his

homework and he effectively sewed up all the arguments about what the machine might or might not do. After a briefing session with him on the probable cost of the whole operation, and a delicate interrogation on what other hidden problems the installation of the machines might cough up, we held a council of war and both Ned and me came to the conclusion that in this machine, we had a 'hot potato'.

Management were reluctant to budge from a position which Her Majesty's Government had underlined of the percentage payment, and we could only see trouble ahead. With the Annual Works Holiday looming and the promise of plenty of overtime and fat wage packets, the sunny beaches of Portugal seemed infinitely preferable to the men than standing by any principle.

The next stage was a visit to the Works manager in the company of Sam and George. The manager was a north countryman, and every feature of his face seemed to reflect the raw, uncompromising bareness of the moors. Immaculately groomed, his piercing blue eyes bored into mine as we were formally introduced and, momentarily, I was thrown off balance by the gutteral welcome. He was a man to be treated with the same degree of caution as handling prussic acid.

Flanked by lesser dignitaries, with bulges in their hip pockets betraying not berettas but pocket calculators, the manager's office had that certain atmosphere one associates with cathedrals, hospitals and doctors' waiting rooms – humbling and *tense*.

I began a silent, mental justification of our case. Being well aware that the railways were £60,000,000 in the red and the prospect of doubling commuter fares, with the loss of 40,000 jobs and 2,000 miles of track, did not create an atmosphere of optimism from our point of view. However, our industry had had a forty per cent reduction in staff in the past ten years *without* industrial trouble, and all we were asking for was the rate for the job. Our business was to sell our labour on an open market and we were certainly

34

not intending to undervalue our expertise.

The Works manager began in a minor key by outlining the advantages of the Data Capture machine, the predictable spiel about British Rail being in the forefront of advanced technology, and so on. Then came the crunch.

'What will be the remuneration for operating the machines?' enquired Ned. The manager adopted the look of a startled fawn — hurt, surprised, wounded to the quick. 'What do you mean?' he gasped. *'Remuneration . . .?'* And he turned to the chief clerk in mock surprise and enquired, 'What *do* they mean?'

Sam interjected quietly and with studied deliberation, 'What they mean is that they want more money for operating the machines and that's what we've come here to discuss . . .'

And once again we were on the familiar bandwagon concerning where final responsibility for processing the data lay. This was a theme which was to become as monotonous and compulsive as eating peanuts in the weeks and months to come. Future meetings developed along the same lines. There was the same case, the same script, the same finale. No money from their side, no deal from ours.

But, in the following weeks, a subtle form of strategy was adopted by management. The boss visited the factory floor and by an entirely undemocratic method, succeeded in dividing the opinion of the men. With the prospect of those sunny beaches on the horizon and the inducement of overtime, he packaged his goodies most attractively. There were promises of higher grades if the machines were operated and redundancy if they weren't, and with calculated sophistry and sycophancy, he split the ranks and the issue was decided on a single vote: the machines were to be operated with a pay differential of seventy-two pence, pending negotiations and a decision taking place at National level. So be it. I took the philosophic view that 'you can't win 'em all'.

The seventy-two pence fell far short of the five pounds

differential but the men had accepted the figure on a temporary basis while a Joint Enquiry, composed of British Rail Engineering Ltd management and NUR full-time officials, conducted an on-site investigation into our claim. However, having backed this particular horse into the stable, British Rail weren't going to leave the door unlocked. A flood of instructions followed in the wake of the machines being operated and a systematic, irreversible logic flowed from that point in time: there was to be no going back to the old manual system of operating the department.

Over a period, the old hands began to quake in expectation of the dire consequences if the wrong buttons were pushed. Some were understandably afraid they would not be able to cope with the new-fangled methods and so they took refuge in consoling each other. The younger men were, on the whole, less conscientious, more flexible; their attitude was 'we'll give it a try, if it doesn't suit we can always jack the job in and find another.' At this particular time their reasoning was well-grounded as the town was ideally situated so far as employment was concerned. These days 'options' would be very thin on the ground, but then there were vacancies at all the local engineering works, and so the attitude of the two age groups in the face of impending change was polarized.

The generation that had lived through the war years and the gloomy fifties, and had served the railways for most of their working lives, were apprehensive and averse to change. They had a strong sense of discipline and their loyalty to the firm was markedly higher than that of the younger men. On the other hand, the adaptability and awareness that change was a necessary part of life made the younger element far more plastic to managerial requirements and, inevitably, there was a clear division of opinion on the shop floor. The old hands felt their status and years of experience were being withered away, and the younger blokes were glad to short-circuit the traditional lines of promotion and start on an equal footing.

So, the machines became operational and we awaited a visit from the members of the Joint Enquiry. We were still waiting for the result of the investigation almost twelve months later!

5

On Course

My college had been the public library and I felt that my horizons needed to be widened. There were so many aspects of union and industrial affairs of which I was totally ignorant, and so I applied to go on an industrial day release course. My application was accepted and I was called into the gaffer's office to be briefed. He informed me that I would be required to give a report on the value of the thirty-week course when I had completed it. The report was to include brief comments on the knowledge and skills imparted, aspects of the course of which particular note should be taken, and how the trainee would alter the course-content and make it more enjoyable. I was also handed a paper with a graph designed to assess the value of the thirty-week exercise and this was divided into three parts: Useless, Useful and Very Useful.

Joe put a different interpretation on the matter. 'The big boss isn't too keen on forking out money for blokes to go on this day release course. He thinks they come back with bolshy ideas and that it is detrimental in the long run.'

'Have you been on the course?' I asked him.

'Yes. You'll have a good ol' time, and if you intend to put your back into things it'll do you a lot of good. But if you think it'll be an easy skive then you won't get any benefit and neither will any other beggar.'

And this piece of gutty wisdom I took to heart.

The thirty weeks consisted of lectures and discussions on Economics, English and Industrial Relations. Joe gave me a grilling before I went and his comments, as always, were sage and useful, particularly his penetrating analysis of the value of adult education.

'Remember, there's no way of getting to know owt except through discipline and hard graft, and only you will know how much effort you're intending to put into the next thirty weeks.'

When I spoke to Ned about the venture he snorted and curled his lip. 'Too much education ain't such a good thing. Look what it did for Adam. I do the steward's job by instinct,' he explained. 'I've been on all sorts of courses but I've come to the conclusion that at the end of the day it's a load of codswallop to think you can do this job by the slide-rule technique. A bit of commonsense is superior to anything those long-haired boys from the red-brick universities can tell us.'

So, armed with an exercise book and a headful of hope I embarked on a safari into the higher echelons of education.

It was a rewarding experience to get up at the usual time but prepare for the day at a more leisurely pace. There is much to be said for eating a civilized breakfast at seven-thirty a.m. rather than having one's first meal of the day at nine-thirty; salmon paste sandwiches washed down with a cup of tea in ten minutes isn't good for one's digestion.

The day was sunny and inviting as I made my way through a nobby part of the town to the converted Georgian house that was the headquarters of the Workers' Educational Association. There were about thirty men on the course, all drawn from a variety of unions. We sat in an ante-room exchanging views and the talk was bubbly with enthusiasm for the future weeks. Suddenly, a chap breezed into the room – a gangling young bloke with a Hitler forelock drooping over his left eye. He looked disdainfully over the intake and said in a bored voice, 'OK, answer your name when I call it . . .'

Our names were dutifully answered with a certain respect for such a young man who evidently had such a good job. Good jobs and clip-boards went together in our view.

After this preliminary he said, 'My name is Charlie Richards. If you want to know anything, if you get into any kind of difficulty, I'm the man to see.'

'He's a Commy,' whispered one bloke to his mate on my right.

'How'd you know that?' his mate replied in a *sotto voce*.

'He flogs the *Socialist Worker* outside the Guildhall every Saturday afternoon.'

Charlie Richards continued, 'I hope you all benefit from the events of the next thirty weeks and go away with something useful. As you will note, my accent is Geordie. I've bummed around the world – France, Holland, Germany – you name it, I've been there and I've done it. One thing life has taught me, 'n that's for sure: the further you get away from Newcastle, the weaker the beer gets.'

We grinned and my grin muffled a groan. My visions of the dreaming spires of Oxford began to grow increasingly dim from that moment onwards.

It was certainly strange to sit at a desk, with the sun streaming through the windows, a virginal sheet of white paper before me, biro poised. I went back in time to 1939. Then I was thirteen years of age and that was the last time I sat at a desk. There were over thirty years between me and a formal education.

I took to the English tutor right away. She was in her late fifties, a spinster, tweedy, and to the point. Teaching was her bread and butter and she communicated her enthusiasm for her subject. I was in my element when she conducted us through the mysteries of the procedure in the local library and we were introduced to the various services and facilities. When the opportunity presented itself I raised the question of the Christian faith, hoping that beneath the polished enunciation and middle class imperturbability there might be a dynamic member of the Mothers' Union, or a zippy Pentecostal piano-player. I was disappointed. Instead I was treated to a benevolent smile and an explanation that she was a convinced agnostic. The rest of the blokes on the course also began to have their doubts about me especially when, having escaped from the budgie-like chatter and fag-smoke, I found myself a quiet corner and read the *Daily Telegraph*.

When we were asked what newspaper we read and why, I told them I read the *Telegraph* because I was a masochist.

The Economics lecturer was a frigid character who personified the parlous state of the nation's economy. Gloom and despondency and a certain nihilism pervaded his lectures.

The Industrial Relations tutor was a different kettle of fish and a mutual antipathy existed between us. He was avant-garde and betrayed his politics with his Chinese cap, red shirt and goatee beard. Bolshy and brash, he would propel his five-feet and two inches into the lecture room and, with his dirty raincoat flapping behind him like a startled hen, fling his heavy briefcase on the desk with a resounding bump. Then his eyes would sweep over his charges and he'd slowly grin, creating the impression that we were all boys together. He was a matey lecturer who, having delivered a broadside of incontrovertible fact, would fasten it in our brains by rapping out, 'Got it? OK?'

I hadn't got it and I wasn't OK. The only true ideal in my mind for a just society is a theocracy, and being a classical pre-millenarian and in line with the Reformers, anything less than that was, at best, a compromise. I also became increasingly fed up listening to the gospel according to Marx during the free discussion sessions.

I was further disillusioned when the statistical credibility of a set of figures was questioned and weirdly shown to be entirely a matter of convenience. Figures regarding payment for the job could be manipulated by union and management and the same figures could have very different meanings. This latter piece of information hit the class with the force of a revelation from heaven. The tutor allowed a chip of his smile to fall off so that it became a leer and said, 'Now you can go back and baffle the gaffers with that one!'

His profanities and square-wheel humour caused my adrenalin to bubble and his evident sympathy with everything I was opposed to – abortion, euthanasia, evolution – were flashpoint issues, somehow prised into the lectures and did nothing to improve *our* particular corner of industrial relations. After a particularly gruelling session, I went home and told Pat. She listened sympathetically nodding her head at the right intervals.

'You see,' I said, 'I feel *trapped*. I don't feel able to cope with these whizz kids.'

'I think you ought to consider pulling out of the thing altogether,' she said. 'After all, I've got to live with you!'

Pat's analysis of the situation was absolutely right: I decided to opt out. I felt my Christianity had come to a crucial testing point. Short of challenging the man on fundamental issues in an open lecture, and thereby disrupting the class and leaving a nasty deposit, the only alternative was to withdraw quietly. Perhaps I was getting too long in the tooth to have Christian beliefs so radically challenged in an academic atmosphere. On the shop floor it was different, verbally keel-hauling Christianity didn't get under my skin, but the little fellow with the Chinese cap, goatee beard and dirty, flapping raincoat represented the new and frightening face of the educated ultra-Left.

I suppose there would be some folk in the church who might wonder why I smile whenever I hear pulpiteering cant to the effect that 'One with God is a majority'. No doubt it is but it would be more reassuring to feel it at times.

I prayed and thought hard about the matter and then wrote a letter, sending three copies: one to the secretary of the course, one to my union branch secretary and one to the big boss at the factory. I outlined my reasons for leaving the course with another twenty weeks to run. I did not realize how deep-rooted my convictions were until they were challenged in circumstances which inhibited me. In the final analysis I suppose my eschatological view was influential in determining the course of my action. After all, every Sunday I made a credal statement affirming my belief that Jesus Christ shall come to judge the living and the dead, and that the body will be resurrected. A whole body of doctrine flows from these statements. To have such beliefs challenged in open debate was one thing, but to have them systematically and quietly undermined, without the opportunity to answer back, was another.

My decision caused a minor shock wave and I felt an even keener sense of isolation from my colleagues. Moreover, I could sympathize with their view of the situation and readily appreciate how difficult it was for them to understand my point of view. Sam and George were tight lipped and a little sour; after all, they felt I'd let the side down. The secretary of the course was courteous but puzzled. Ned was testy and perplexed. However, my decision did create the opportunity to have a talk with the big boss.

My dealings with him up to that moment had been strictly circumscribed by the dispute regarding payment for operating the Data Capture machines. But, as I subsequently discovered, he was a totally different person from the shifty boss-class, calculating character I had come to regard with the greatest suspicion.

When I was asked to give a report to him about the day release course and my decision to opt out I felt his motives were questionable. My honest evaluation of the course ratified his view that it was merely an expensive exercise in State-subsidized industrial sabotage, and it was in this vein that he carried on a monologue for twenty minutes. Then he said, 'I'm a Christian y'know,' and then confidentially, 'I know you go to church!'

Suddenly, the man ceased to be Captain of Industry, controlling the lives of four thousand of his fellows, and he became a thoughtful, quiet reflective man sharing something of his hopes and fears and the understanding he had of Jesus Christ and the Church.

The original zeal of his early Methodist origins had become a tired affiliation to a sleepy Church of England which, he vehemently insisted, bore no resemblance to his early experience of the Church. I was quick to assure him that I too was Church of England but my 'home' church did not correspond with the depressing picture he painted of the one he attended.

'Look,' I said, quite unconscious of the fact he was the boss, 'I belong to a charismatic church which has a special ministry to the down-and-outs and those considered the dregs of society. Unless we're prepared to get alongside people *where* they are – not where we'd like them to be – and feel something of the withdrawal symptoms of someone like the drug addict, and know the hunger for wholeness in the heart of a prostitute, then we're not measuring up to the demands of the Gospel of Jesus Christ.'

He grunted, 'You're right of course, but tell me,' and here he looked at his watch, 'it's now three-thirty and Friday afternoon. If I walk through the shops on these works now, I'll see dozens of men sitting down doing nothing. They think the working week finishes at starting time on the Friday afternoon shift. If I kick their pants I'll be called a rotten beggar. How would *you* set about convincing the men in this factory that to work an honest eight hour day is the answer to most of our problems?'

I felt my hackles beginning to rise. 'It's not only the blokes on the factory floor. The problem is more deep-rooted than that. It's the whole of our society, not one section. If we relegate sin to a theological proposition and fail to see it as the core of human nature without God then we aren't reading the situation right!'

There was a moment's silence. Then he abruptly reached for a file and said, 'That man Goldsmith, he has been having two days a week off for months and bringing in sick-notes with all kinds of reasons for his absence. I think the man's a walking miracle!' And then facetiously: 'Do you think I ought to sack him?'

Once again he was the boss-man. 'No sir,' I replied, 'have a talk to him.'

'A *fatherly* talk?'

'A *fatherly* talk sir.'

'The last time I had one of your chaps up here I took him through the Garden of Gethsemane, remember?'

'I remember. I had the job of convincing him that management can't just sack a bloke without very good reason and in his case, the reasons weren't justifiable. You can't sack a bloke for revving a fork-lift truck outside the gaffer's office and stinking his place out with diesel fumes. With respect, you scared him stiff when you read the riot act over to him!'

'You do think I led him through Gethsemane's Garden?'

'You almost took the bloke to Golgotha!' and in that moment I bit my tongue and felt like Judas.

The keen sensitivity to spiritual values was becoming blunted and I knew it. Although I might have found it difficult to articulate, I realized that I was becoming more coarse-grained in my outlook on life. It is the little foxes that spoil the tender vine and I saw that in my heart I was becoming distanced from the Christ I knew at the beginning of my spiritual pilgrimage.

The quiet erosion continued. The stand I took on so many minor issues was uneasily justified. A flamboyant gesture of disapproval such as withdrawing from the course was easy to establish but, for example, being taken into confidence by the management in their endeavour to wear a man down so that he asked for demotion was a matter which troubled me. Perhaps management had a good case, maybe the man was a malingerer, or a bad timekeeper, and so if there was insufficient hard evidence to back their judgement then a subtle strategy might be adopted.

The options were simple, either one went along with management's connivings or one condoned the 'bad' employee's behaviour and argued against demotion. A neutral position was an anathema and an abdication of one's responsibilities. But it wasn't easy to identify where those responsibilities lay.

In church discussion groups it was easy to pin moral values on contrived and artificial situations. Hard questions were generally shunted into a siding and left strictly alone.

To debate the latest theological book on 'The Nature of Work' may be stimulating and helpful, but next day one had to come down from the upper storey and argue the case of a dozen men who refused to touch a wagon loaded with axleboxes because the load was dangerous or dirty. As their representative I came down on their side every time because I've handled those wagons and paying demurrage on a wagon under dispute is cheaper in my book than losing a leg.

Perhaps the finishing touch was provided by the lecturer who, on my last day on the course said, 'Now, it'll do us good to get out and about next Tuesday so we'll all go to Letford University to look at their library. The taxpayer will be footing the bill and they've got good recreational facilities there, so if you see anybody hanging around looking like a statue, don't worry, he'll be a student like yourselves!'

6

The Clockwatchers

Random sampling is a device used by work study engineers to determine how much time is gainfully occupied. Under an agreement between the management and the union, we were obliged to accommodate these characters with clipboards and stopwatches. In my experience, when a young tradesman decides to sling his overalls and become a work study engineer trainee, two things happen. First he sartorially improves his appearance and second, he forgets to smile. The transition from being a matey sort of chap with an infectious zest for life to a taciturn, serious-minded bloke is rapid and permanent and can only be the result of his change of occupation.

When I was informed that a six-week random sample was to be conducted on the department I was a little apprehensive. I had had first hand experience of being the subject of some scrutiny on the part of the random samplers and the only comfort this time was that I was shop steward and could exercise some leverage.

When the news was 'leaked' that the exercise was due to take place, Ned and me were subjected to a barrage of criticism. Why couldn't we stop it? Whose idea was it anyway? Was management out to cut staff and if so, what action did we advocate? Was the whole thing tied up with the introduction of the Data Capture machine? What about that flamin' computer — when would that Joint Enquiry take place, and was the sample taking into account the wholesale alteration in our work-pattern? Why didn't the bleedin' samplers go where all work study engineers ultimately went . . . And so on.

The truth was, we had no power to stop the exercise; we could only argue a good case for staving off the inevitable and the only case we could put forward was the fluid situation of the work load and the process of reorganization that was taking place. This argument had been successfully used on more than one occasion and armed with the argument of precedent we tried to convince management of the futility of conducting a sample.

No luck. A gritty, slant-eyed, heavy-jowled top gaffer in a Hector Powe suit shuffled the papers on his desk and read out the appropriate minute that clobbered our plea for 'more time' stone dead.

We talked to the lads on the shop floor and tried to placate their fears. The sample, we said, was simply an artifice of management's convenience to find out where the heaviest work load was and what might be the manpower requirements in the future. And in any case, a random sample was much better than a full work study, with the clock and clipboard. Going to the lavatory and knowing somebody was outside timing the operation was, to say the least, undignified.

For the purpose of evaluation, the measured working day of 480 minutes incorporates a built-in RA (Relaxation Allowance) and this takes the form of a six-minute break every hour. The ten-minute tea break in the morning is included in the allowance and so also is smoking and going to the lavatory. Subjection to the indignity of the man with the stopwatch is an occupational hazard on the shop floor.

In my view it was much more than plain undignified. It was a violation of my Christian status as a man born in the image of God. To be reduced to the level of a lump of protoplasm and conditioned to perform certain work functions in a pre-determined manner and at a predetermined pace is a denial of the essential God-image and dignity of the working man.

What price is the 'glorify God in your daily work' motto when the measured day doesn't take into account Jack's diarrhoea or old Bill's rheumatism, or the monotony of the job? The professional classes would regard a man with a stopwatch, monitoring their movements every minute of the working day, with the utmost resentment and could probably articulate that resentment in a constructive way. On the shop floor, however, there could well be a build-up of aggravation and rebellion against the system which employs one set of rules for the gaffers and an entirely different one for the men. A strike or go-slow might be the only method whereby the feeling of the men might be forcibly brought home to the bosses.

The random samplers had their observation times drawn out of a computer to 'ensure absolute fairness' and this mindless contraption even decanted that the observations take place during the hallowed dinner-break, after the men had clocked out. Needless to say, the unfortunate samplers were subjected to a good deal of abuse in spite of their apologetic assurances that the observations during this period 'didn't count'.

The six week sample was regarded by the men as a challenge to their ingenuity and their attitude was, 'if the management are playing at spy, then we'll enter into the spirit of the game'. Their inventive genius was remarkable and Hoodwinking the Samplers was a pastime freely indulged in by all.

One enterprising gang – A gang – laid a three-hundred yard 'telegraph' of copper wire and appointed one of their number to act as an observer in an elaborate early warning system. He would be on the outer perimeter mechanically chucking bolts into a trailer and taking his time while watching for the 'enemy'. When a couple of neat suits appeared on the horizon, complete with their time sheets and stopwatches, the wire would be pulled and two lumps of iron at the other end would clang together. When the two 'spies' eventually approached the gang from two different observation points they observed a hive of industry. Not a *Mirror* or a *Sun* in sight, the mashing cans washed and ready for the official tea-break, and not a trace of a crafty sit-down and smoke. According to the findings of the samplers, A gang should have been sent to Russia to show the stakhanovite workers the meaning of dedicated labour.

Another character hit on the idea of suspending a barrel on a pulley and chain and when the 'enemy' was sighted from a convenient vantage point, the barrel would be arduously lowered, or lifted, just as the samplers made their appearance.

Wagons took longer to unload under the sampler's eye – the lads certainly weren't going to work themselves out of a job by buckling in and emptying the wagon in the normal way. Ordinarily, they were able to knock off and have a smoke after the uncongenial and heavy task of sorting out a mixed load of springs, steel plates, axleboxes and all manner of ironwork associated with the making and repairing of rolling stock. Grease, muck and the odd injury were part of the labourers' normal working day and, quite rightly, they considered that if a wagon had been loaded by mechanical means with no consideration given to careful separating for transportation and stacking, then they were entitled to a 'spit and a draw' after unloading.

A punctilious sampler didn't see things that way at all and the opposition to their presence took the form of calculated deceit.

Quite a number of the older hands took exception to the poor young fellows with the stopwatches. They were suspicious of their rosy-cheeked innocence, mounted in stiff white collars. These youngsters were ignorant of the days when there were no fork-lift trucks and cranes and all the ironwork had to be manhandled. Now things were easier, but it was the poor old labourer who was the target for cutbacks and layoffs. Whether this attitude was right or wrong was merely an academic question. The fact was that they were being observed, and they resented it. The acrimony was further ventilated by the option granted to the employee to question the observations of the samplers and complain to the chief work study engineer if he thought an observation was unfair or biased. Having the right to challenge the 'enemy' had built-in complications and I spent a good deal of time in putting out potential bushfires as tempers reached flashpoint. We did experience a difficulty in handling one hard line old-timer who made it perfectly clear that so far as he was concerned the 'stop watch men can stop watchin' me because they ain't workin' – which meant that he sat down and twiddled his thumbs whenever the observers were around. It was an eccentric, negative, perfectly understandable and gloriously English way of combating what is patently a ridiculous and false method of evaluating men at work. Even so with a little persuasion, the recalcitrant old boy was brought back into line and made to see the folly and futility of his ways.

When the samplers' figures were ultimately released the absurdity of the six-week operation was manifest for all to see. The men themselves knew where the work load was heaviest. They were familiar with the labour force. The lead-swingers, the workshy, the skivers and grafters were all part of their working lives and when the findings were released it was apparent that many of the blokes had missed their vocation – they should have been playing dramatic roles at the Old Vic. Areas which had a comparatively light work load had the same work content percentage as other areas we *knew* to be fully extended. The only conclusion was that the men had been successful in defeating the system.

It may be argued that the men themselves manipulated the findings and the artificial figures were the result of their uncooperative attitude and calculated deceit, but if the morality of random sampling is in question – as I believe it is – then the men were completely justified and could not be blamed for adopting a negative attitude. I admit that I did feel a pang of conscience in condoning such action, but I wondered, even at the time, whether this was the result of long conditioning to a middle-class conception of what is 'Christian' and what is 'carnal'. In any case I had been on the receiving end of the sampler's observations. I had been one of those statistical points. Consequently I felt a keen sense of satisfaction in throwing a spanner into the works.

On the other hand, as a Christian I wondered whether I should have adopted a more passive role and submitted to what I believed to be a most unjust practice on the part of my employers.

7

Cameos and Characters

There was another aspect of life on the shop floor which was particularly the preserve of the shop steward, and one that I highly valued.

O. Henry, the American short-story writer, once said that if he wanted an idea for a short story, all he had to do was to knock on the door of the first house in any street and say to the occupant, 'Flee for your life, all is found out!' It was true. Many of the men I worked alongside had problems they wanted to share with someone. The ministry of the open ear was a very necessary part of my duties, and the problems were as varied as the men. The shop steward was regarded as a lightning conductor for personal difficulties, the recounting of which might have proved embarrassing to officialdom. The parish priest was a distant figure out on the periphery. Indeed, the institutional church was seldom mentioned in the context of dealing with personal issues, and the Citizens Advice Bureau was shunned as an antiseptic arm of the Welfare State.

I found myself fulfilling the role of adviser to many of the men. I made full use of my church connections – professional people who were Christians and ready to give practical help and advice. It was very rewarding and gave me a good deal of satisfaction. In these situations, my conscience and moral scruples were not salvaged by having to play the devil's advocate and argue cases that were not only lost but completely unjustifiable – bad timekeeping, for example, without a reasonable excuse.

Billy for instance was thin, small and undernourished.

He had lived in a small terraced house with his mother and when she died, his world collapsed. At forty-three years of age he considered that life had passed him by. An inherent and debilitating shyness had inhibited any question of meeting a member of the opposite sex and his only relative was a sister who lived in Australia. So, Billy, who had worked for the railway since leaving the army, began to lose all interest in life.

The planning authority decided to pull down the rows of terraced houses where Billy had lived all his life and re-house the inhabitants in high-rise flats on the outskirts of town. Although Billy had 'nothing to do with neighbours' regarding them as 'nosy parkers', he did resent the upheaval of moving from the old and familiar. In Billy's view, the 'social engineers' ought to have regarded his situation in a more beneficent light. After all, the two-up and two-down with its outside privy and cockroaches crawling up the kitchen wall may have been dirty but it was *friendly* and *comfortable*. Besides, it was *his* house, bought for three-hundred quid after the war and Billy could sit under his own vine and relish his lonely misery in the security of a familiar environment.

The borough council was very much in favour of every man sitting under his own vine but the particular locality of Billy's new vine was eighteen floors up, with a concrete balcony scything a skyline made up of a dozen other phallic tower blocks.

He had no need to worry about neighbours being nosy; there was an antiseptic indifference on the part of the flat dwellers to any social contact with each other. After a few weeks in his new surroundings Billy developed a melancholy outlook on life; he became very depressed and spoke of death as a happy release. The immediate view from his flat on the eighteenth floor didn't help matters, the high-rise buildings, the mushroom of small factories on an industrial estate, and away in the distance the Crescendo Sports Centre – the crowning glory of the town. Thirty-two storeys high with bingo, skittles, roller skating, two swimming pools, indoor tennis courts and a spinning cafe on the top to catch the sun.

Billy was sick of the flat.

With a curious blend of principled regard for his job as a packer and a fatalistic disregard for his welfare, Billy began to deteriorate physically and mentally. He steadfastly refused to see a doctor, in spite of what he called 'the shakes' – a distressing series of convulsions in which his whole body shook, coupled with a hacking cough and shortness of breath.

I visited him every morning at work in the small cubbyhole constructed of packing cases and well out of sight of the gaffer's eye. His frail body would palpitate as he sucked his Players and always a small bottle of whisky stood within handy reach. His melancholia seemed to evaporate as he settled down on his stool, his transistor softly playing and the *Racing Tipster* spread out on a wooden box that served as a table. A bevy of mice was almost on speaking terms with Billy; when things were quiet they'd frolic in the dark corners. He also had a picture of the Queen pinned above his head and a poster extolling the virtues of the Conservative Party.

Very often he would be totally insulated from the world around him and when in a particularly depressed state, he rarely spoke to anyone. In such circumstances it is easy to see how someone like Billy, working in a large nationalized concern, can become submerged into the background unnoticed . . . forgotten.

A deposit of matriarchal tradition was very evident in his political views: 'The Tory Party is the only cussin' party that cares – that's what me poor old mum used to say and she was cussin' well right.'

Equally unorthodox was his evaluation of his menial job: 'No beggar can pack like me with all me experience . . .' and then he would reflect on his life and his loneliness and he'd finish his soliloquy, '. . . and I'm only fit for the knackers yard'.

He was suspicious of the Church and resented any suggestion that maybe he'd like a visit from the minister.

When he absented himself from work for three days I went to his flat.

It was a bleak February night and the wind sighed weird songs as it swept around the tower block. I walked along the corridor on the eighteenth floor and sensed something of that alienation and loneliness that Billy had often spoken about. The feeling was akin to the one I had experienced on the escalator in the London underground, during the rush hour, when I saw the faces of the people moving in the opposite direction. Like human battery hens, intent on their own business, blank, humourless, making their way from tin boxes underneath to concrete boxes on top, emotionally insulated from each other . . . The quiet corridor had an atmosphere of cultivated decay.

I knocked at number twenty-three, and the door slowly, cautiously opened. Billy, his face a ghastly pallor in the half-light, peered questioningly at me.

'What can I do for you?' he asked.

'I've just come to see if you're alright,' I replied.

There was a moment's silence as he deliberated what to do and eventually he said, 'You'd better come in.'

Billy's decor had taken something of the shine away from the brassy, twentieth-century functionalism of the flat. Sepia photographs of Dad and Mam strutted across the low shelf above the radiator ('I never switch that cussin' thing on – it eats money') and two horses stood on a seashore encased in a fading gold frame while a wild wind blew in from the sea. Majestic flower pots, in which lolled plastic roses, decorated an old fashioned sideboard, and an old Marconi wireless-set in a heavy mahogany cabinet with mastodon-like feet stood in a corner. On a solid, no-nonsense kitchen table was spread a plastic tablecloth and the only source of heat in the room was a two-bar electric fire. The room had that certain foetid

56

cabbage smell. Billy wore an old Tootal, long dressing gown which he later informed me he had bought from Oxfam for half-a-crown ('which is Christian money not like this continental metric muck!'). He gestured me to sit in a high-backed chair and eventually spoke. 'I'm feelin' bad. I got the shakes. I ought to pack up the fags. Only the whisky keeps me going . . .'

'Is there anything I can do for you Billy?' I asked, half-fearing his proud independence might be violated if I sounded too concerned.

'Yes, there is somethin' you can do,' he emphatically declared. 'My job, I don't want *anybody* on my job. I'm goin' to the doctor's tomorrow. He gives me pills. They don't do me much good 'cos I'm due for the knacker's yard but the main thing is me job, you just can't put any cussin' fool on packin'. I want to get back to work. Just make sure they don't put *anybody* on my job . . .'

Next day I went to see the gaffer about Billy. He was sympathetic but pointed out he was running a factory and not a convalescent home. I promised to monitor Billy's performance at work and generally look after his interests.

It wasn't long before Billy was back in harness. The factory was the only place where he had any status or a stake in society. There were the people who spoke to him and with whom he felt secure. There he had a reason for living, but soon his physical condition began to worsen rapidly.

A few weeks later I called in the newspaper shop for my morning paper. George behind the counter said, 'You ought to have been here ten minutes ago.'

'Why?' I replied.

'The little bloke, Billy. 'E collapsed and my missus went to phone for an ambulance, but before anybody could do anything, Billy was gorn. I picked 'im up an' it was like pickin' up a doll. No weight, 'n 'is face was like wax, poor little gonner.'

The funeral took place a few days later. It was a cold

March morning and the louring skies wept copious tears. We sat in the crematorium chapel. Two neighbours, women, hatchet-faced and sombre, with a predilection for visiting the crematorium at every decent opportunity sat a respectable distance from the front, and four of us – Billy's workmates – sat behind them.

The minister whose tour of duty it was officiated and efficiently piloted Billy on his last ride. He recited the sober words of the burial service in a flat, neutral voice and we sang a couple of appropriate hymns. The small coffin would have easily fitted on the back seat of a mini and a sprig of flowers rested on top. As was customary, we had collected at work and sent along a spray of daffs and they nodded their heads in sympathy as Billy moved on his last journey. The red velvet curtains swished together and he slid out of sight.

Billy is not an isolated case by any means. All the ingredients of Billy's life are shared among many workers in the factory. Loneliness, the feeling of rejection, personal tragedy that has left deep and crippling effects on a man's personality . . . Charlie for example.

Charlie hadn't been away on a holiday for many years because he was devoted to his boy who had suffered a brain injury during a minor operation on his tonsils. The laddie had been in a comatose state for all this time and Charlie carried his burden with rare courage. His wife found it increasingly difficult to cope, but Charlie nudged his way through life with a bluff, rough, coarse-grained humour and a ready acceptance of the 'way things have turned out'. The heartache, the bitterness, the weariness all found an outlet in his dirty sense of humour and overbearing manner.

Meeting Charlie for the first time might well be a repelling experience. He is a big man, lantern-jawed with steely-grey eyes that have a tendency to narrow menacingly when authority, in any guise, is in question. Furthermore, unshockability is a necessary prerequisite where

Charlie is concerned. If the dilettantes on the telly have, like little schoolboys, discovered that four letter words are naughty and in vogue, then Charlie could bridge a semantic gap and offer umpteen variations wholly original of the classical obscenities.

Herbert, another bloke in the factory, suffered from epilepsy and found his malady a most embarrassing and distressing inconvenience. He was convinced his illness was the reason why he had been passed over for promotion. He wrote beautiful poetry and regarded his literary talent as the one way by which he would break loose of the railway industry. He detested his job with an almost pathological indifference as to what might happen to himself and his family should he suddenly decide to ask for his cards. With a mournful disposition, he had come to terms with the fact that May, his wife, didn't *mean* to henpeck him and behave so abominably towards him . . .

It was Herbert who brought me perhaps my most perplexing problem. He came to me one day with a worried look on his face. It seems that just after the war his sister married an American GI and settled in the USA. The early post-war years were times of austerity and rationing and his sister had taken pity on Herbert and the rest of the family back in poor old England. She expressed her concern in a very loving and practical way by sending a huge food parcel every Christmas. As an added treat she also packed a carefully prepared selection of ingredients for a Christmas cake. Every year the parcel arrived faithfully but Herbert confessed he had certain misgivings when the last one was deposited at his address. The contents were carefully checked and, indeed, all the ingredients for the cake were there including a small package of grey powder which Herbert and his wife thought was seasoning for the cake. May made the cake.

'A beauty it was,' said Herbert. 'Took five hours to cook and when it came out of the oven you could have fed on the smell. We packed the cake in a tin so that it might mature for Christmas and a week later we received a letter from my sister which gave May a nasty turn'.

'What was it?' I anxiously enquired.

Herbert paused. 'That's what I've come to see you about. It's a ticklish problem. You remember the little packet of grey powder I spoke about and which we thought was seasoning?'

'Yes.'

'Well, it wasn't seasoning. You see, my sister's father-in-law, Pop, had family ties in England and he died a few months ago and expressed a wish that some of his ashes be scattered in any English field. The 'seasoning' was Pop's ashes, and now', he added pathetically, 'he's part of the Christmas cake.'

I pondered this one thoughtfully. 'What does your missus think?' I asked diplomatically.

'She's rather upset. She says she can't bear to *look* at the cake let alone eat it. She says that to eat it would be cannibalistic. If we scatter the cake the birds will probably eat it and that would be kind of – irreverent – for poor old Pop. What would you do?'

'The only decent thing to do would be to bury it I suppose.'

'I thought you'd say that. Do you think we ought to hold a little service of remembrance? I mean, the cake *is* more than a few crumbs!'

'I don't think so. Just think how happy the old boy would be if he knew he was part of Christmas . . .'

I was regarded as a walking jobcentre by quite a few folk at church, and was often approached with a view to obtaining employment for various individuals. I had a number of disappointing and frustrating experiences with blokes on whose behalf I had approached the management and secured jobs. Johnny for example.

In hindsight, Johnny was congenitally incapable of holding down a job. He was a self-appointed itinerant prophet whose particular calling included Putting The Church

Right. If the prophet's function is to disturb people with The Message then Johnny very competently fulfilled this part of his office.

He had drifted into the church looking like a disaster waiting to happen and the minister had taken pity and fed and clothed him. Having satisfied himself that Johnny was prepared to settle down and lead a 'normal' Christian life and curtail his fire-raising, hell-shaking ministry which had disturbed many people in the church, the minister asked me to see if I could get him a job. I approached the boss and Johnny was duly employed as a labourer.

It would be charitable to pass over and draw a veil on Johnny's subsequent behaviour in the factory. The sad truth was that Johnny needed to be helped and the shop floor was not the most beneficial therapy. His propheteering didn't cut any ice with the men, and his antics caused a great disservice to the cause of Christ. When he was holding forth to a group of blokes on some obscure passage in the minor prophets – in the gaffer's time – and creating a good deal of hilarity with his fervent gesticulations, I overcame my initial embarrassment, took him aside and tried to point out the weakness of his witness. But he regarded me as a Laodicean Christian: I wasn't 'all out'.

He had secured lodgings with a mate of mine – a Christian who was a fitter in the works. One day, my mate came to me with a deeply-furrowed brow.

'This character, Johnny – you've got to do something Ralph. The other night he was talking to me and it was way past midnight and I fell asleep. Next thing I knew, Johnny was laying hands on me to cure me of my tiredness. Another thing, you know that series of meetings we've been having at the church to "bring out your potential"? Well, there was a sort of middle-class play acting with bricks, and the idea was that we had a pile of these bricks and we had to make something out of them. There were three teams and somebody from another team kept pinching our bricks. Next thing, Johnny started to lay hands on this guy because he said the bloke needed delivering from his pinching potential. Now Ralph, I'm desperate. I can't go on living with this super-spiritual guy on cloud nine.'

I promised to have a talk to Johnny and do all in my power to deflect him from his self-appointed mission but, providentially, Johnny's brief but colourful career was swallowed up in a larger light. He suddenly felt called to go and live in a Christian commune somewhere in Bedfordshire where they ate grapenuts on principle, and drank only de-fluoridated water.

Even with Johnny gone, we still had our fair share of characters in the Works – blokes who knew a nod was as good as a wink, whatever the circumstances. The more enterprising among them ran a very convenient shopping service. One could purchase a pound of bacon, lay a bet, buy a packet of contraceptives, order a three piece suite, buy batteries, socks, tea – almost any commodity – on the factory premises. One local boy made good by buying sugar from the local *Co-op* claiming 'divi' on the purchase and charging his workmates a half-penny extra for 'conveyancy' charges. Of course, the management took a dim view of this activity and repeatedly stuck up notices blacking the whole thing and threatening disciplinary action against offenders. However, implementing that course of action was easier said than done. After all, it was a *service* in the men's view and if the gaffer ran short of fags, well, Duggie had his 'shop' where his favourite brand could be purchased.

There were also the barbers' shops where a surreptitious trim at a cheap price could be obtained. Alf, for instance, operated his tonsorial skill in a quiet corner of the yard. 'Can you *do* me?' one would enquire, and Alf would state his time.

The arrangements and timing were as precise as a rocket lift-off. The gaffers would be out of sight – probably supping tea in the foreman's canteen – and one would sit on an upturned box with an unhygienic bit of rag hurriedly bundled around one's neck. Alf would drop fag-ash down the back of the candidate's head as he plied his trade. Alf's eyesight wasn't too good either so he would move his clippers by instinct. He had a kind of built in range-finder and managed to circumvent the ear-lobe by some mysterious sixth sense. Of course, there was no electricity laid on and Alf used nine inch clippers. Hair cutting was a tense business in Alf's 'shop'.

As the shears clopped off large clumps of hair, Alf would talk about the great issues of the day. Burnley's chances in the League Cup, water prospects in the fishing match, the best pint in town, how much the next pay rise was really worth, and so on. All in all, Alf's shop was a no-nonsense establishment. None of your fancy-smelling, chrome-plated tins of green grease and tarty-smelling muck; none of your lilac-overalled lackeys obsequiously giving the Uriah Heep treatment: 'What style sir?' There was only one style: short back and sides. If a gaffer turned up unexpectedly, then there was a mad scramble, and one unfortunate character would wear a trilby for a fortnight. One comb, one pair of shears, one pair of scissors; and when the operation was completed all utensils were folded up in a dirty towel ready for the next session.

Dear old Alf with a nub behind his ear, his watery blue eyes taking a long view from behind his spectacles balanced on the tip of his nose; the disorganized snuff-encrusted wispy moustache and the reedy voice: 'Short back and sides, cock?'

The floor would be covered like a carpet in the after-birth of his trade – brown, black, grey, auburn, ginger. And after the cut, a couple of bob would exchange hands.

The Hairdressers' Federation would sally into this area of extra-industrial activity and howl in their misery about the cowboys taking their bread and butter, and the unhygienic characters who were running foul of the law and foul of the great brotherhood of union members. But Alf still carried on his trade. His was a case of demand and supply. The older hands, at least, were not so well-thatched, nor unduly bothered about styling, and they gave old Alf all the trade he could manage.

8

In an Ideal World . . .

The Church is hard up when it comes to finding Christian shop stewards to invite to 'say a few words about your function in industry'. There is a plethora of teachers and doctors, students and social workers, and the professional middle class more than caters for the needed comments from a Christian perspective on contemporary events. Consequently, the middle class consensus is the only one that comes through; so we have a middle class orientated gospel. This is particularly noticeable in the charismatic movement where the main thrust of evangelical appeal is directed towards an articulate population.

When it was noised abroad that I was a Christian doing a shop steward's job, invitations to address meetings came thick and fast. One felt one was an all purpose plastic figure who fitted into the middle class concept of what the working class was all about. A strong vein of humour, an earthy appraisal of life on the shop floor, speaking the modern 'comfortable words' that Christ had not left himself without a witness in that place . . .

And yet, the misty millions who earn their living on the factory floor are the least touched by the evangel. Why is this? My stint as a shop steward convinced me that one of the primary reasons is this: the Church can find no cultural middle-ground in which to develop and exploit its message. The Church can address itself with ease to the drug addicts, the pill pushers and pill takers, the alcoholics, prostitutes and misfits of our society. But the factory floor remains a no-go area so far as organizational Christianity is concerned. Perhaps it is because we are inclined to think that the great mass of people who work in factories represent a positively boring and predicatable area of human life. Their virtues are not worth mentioning and their vices are dully pedestrian, plain for all to see. Indeed, the social system we have created, which determines what resources will be used for, how things are produced, and who gets what, has neatly packaged and categorized the industrial worker into an instantly recognized article.

As a society, we do not draw our leaders from the State comprehensives. And on the factory floor we take the rejects – the fifteen year olds with little academic ability who have failed in their school life – and we put them on a lathe; whilst those with suitable qualifications are siphoned off into non-industrial careers and occupations. Consequently, on the shop floor we have a broad spectrum of the working class who can safely be categorized.

They read the *Sun* and the *Mirror* and, in the football season, the hot topic of conversation on Monday morning is the match that took place on Saturday. Tempers become frayed when players' ability, lack of opportunity, or stupidity is discussed. In fact, football seems to have largely taken the place of the Church in the religious outlook on the shop floor. There are all the elements of religious devotion: the dedicated chanting on the terraces, the wearing of special clothing, the grief and anxiety which is identified with the local team's form, the shared experience.

And then there are the other favourite subjects. Gaffers, the cost of living, particularly as it affects the basics – beer, fags, petrol and car maintenance – these are the topics of conversation in the tea breaks. This is the shop floor, and it is in this area where the Church of Christ *must* meet the challenge.

In all my years of working for British Rail, I had only a passing acquaintance with an industrial chaplain. When the notice was pinned on the board, 'Any employee wanting an interview with the Rev. Crisp, Industrial Chaplain, apply at the Staff Office', I immediately applied. Some two weeks later I was asked by the clerk to 'go and see the vicar bloke'.

We met in a tiny room in the unfamiliar atmosphere of the Works Manager's floor. The chaplain was a taciturn man with tired eyes and a plummy voice.

'What can I do for you?' he asked.

'Nothing,' I replied. 'I just wanted to meet you. I'm a Christian and a shop steward. I go to St Gregory's . . .'

He averted his eyes and fiddled with his cuff and the Church of Jesus Christ seemed to be in a state of extreme embarrassment in that little box room. I felt awkward; he felt ill at ease. Lamely, the conversation limped to a fretful close. He did manage to croak out the glad news that 'the men watched their language when he was around'.

Afterwards, I asked a dozen blokes at random if they had ever met the industrial chaplain and, if not, whether they wanted to do so. They looked at me as though they'd just been told they were on *Candid Camera*.

No doubt, the Rev. Crisp did an excellent and useful job among men who had plucked up courage to visit him with special problems. But for ordinary men with no hang-ups, the Church and the world were as far apart as ever. Moreover, the Church simply did not know how to take the initiative in propagating its message.

We did have a Christian fellowship in the Works and this served a useful purpose in as much as it gave greatly needed moral support to young Christians who felt isolated and up against things. The group met once every month but as they arranged the meeting to take place fifteen minutes after knocking-off time, it wasn't very well supported. Nevertheless, they soldiered on, with a local luminary giving a fifteen minute talk, and a 'brief discussion' afterwards over tea and biscuits. The group largely consisted of 'safe' evangelicals propagating a highly individualistic and pietistic gospel, a kind of pilgrim's progress that said 'good chucks' to Mrs Christian while Mr Christian battled his way manfully to the gates of the celestial city. So be it. There was no liaison between this group and the Rev. Crisp.

In our rapidly accelerating technological society, the beetlebrows and eggheads multiply, and so do society's rejects. As the cultural differences between these opposing factions become more accentuated, it becomes imperative for the Church to address itself to the 'no go' areas in industry and adopt a more radical and realistic approach. If the Church fails in this it will be failing in its function.

I was becoming more and more aware that it is no use the minister transferring the whole responsibility to the Christian worker, saying: 'You are the Church on the shop floor, Christ has put you there. We can't reach your fellow workers in that boring place where they earn their daily bread – but you can!'

The truth is that Christians in industry are not cultural middle-men and my mates needed more than the good Rev. Crisp with his dog collar to authenticate the message. The industrial chaplain, it seemed to me, was only half-dressed in his charcoal grey and clerical collar; he needed a pair of blue dungarees as well, and his parish ought to be a full time occupation. He should exercise his ministry on the factory floor, in that messy area of human life where men are truly themselves. He should be prepared to sweep the floor and to smell cutting oil, but he would not verbally rape his flock by using four-letter words – they would simply despise him for that. He would be a lonely man, but would be sold out on the Kingdom of God and literally living Matthew 5 to 8.

There came the day when my three year term of office as shop steward came to a close. I had already made it known that I was not prepared to stand for re-election, and so the familiar pattern repeated itself. There was the general canvassing for the vacancy and after a good deal of persuasion, two candidates offered themselves . . .

I tried to evaluate, honestly, what had been achieved by

my stand as a Christian shop steward. Apart from damping down one or two potential bush fires of industrial unrest and injecting a dose of Christian charity in the dialogue with management, the profit and loss account looked very much the same as if a good-living atheist had served in the same capacity.

I had experienced something of the sharp cost of discipleship – the conflict of loyalties, the areas of blurred morality; and I had discovered new dimensions of Christian understanding. Relationships which hitherto I might have avoided became richer and more rewarding. Through a shared experience I came to realize that God makes even the wrath of men to praise him, and a love for my fellow worker became much more a reality and less a theological hack-word.

That I was disillusioned in so many ways is probably the result of my inability to be more than a run-of-the-mill Christian, carrying treasure in a badly cracked vessel. My Christian witness on the shop floor may have been idealistically desirable, but for me to be part of the process and to maintain my integrity and subscribe practically to the truth of Christianity; to be frighteningly honest in my dealings with my fellow men (whether men or management) – there was the rub. And my disillusionment grew . . .

9

Moving Out

On 16 January 1979, I opened my eyes: 6.15 a.m. It was a programmed sequence and I needed no mechanical means to wake me. The bedroom was bathed in that ethereal glow which meant we'd had an overnight fall of snow. Pat was still in that twilight zone between waking and sleeping when suddenly I said very deliberately, 'I don't want to go to work!'

There was a brief silence. Then, in a tone of voice guaranteed to unfreeze the Arctic, burning with sincerity and now very wide awake, she replied, 'You don't *honestly* mean that do you?'

Again I said in a very strange, unnatural voice, 'I don't want to go to work.' And I didn't.

For thirty-three years I had worked for British Rail. My job was secure. After all, I'd worked there for the best part of a working life and the railway looked after its own. I had a good wage, an assured pension, seven free rail-passes a year and in a few months time, the choice of a clock, Kenwood mixer or a pair of binoculars being presented to me for 'long and meritorious service'. And that thought bothered me. I couldn't help thinking that there's nothing so secure as a grave – and I felt like a well-kept grave.

I had become a shop steward, not because I felt hot under the collar about the class struggle but I just thought that being a Christian shop steward gave me an extra dimension of living on the shop floor. I mean, how could I reconcile an Abrahamic pilgrimage – looking for the city of God – with counting nuts and bolts? I was a storekeeper but didn't particularly shine at storekeeping. I have a congenital inability to remember, and mathematics has always been my Achilles' heel.

My home life was happy, but had reached a changing point. Pat and I now lived in a detached house with a beautiful detached garden. Our relationship with our two daughters was becoming detached. Ruth was happily married and Eirene was engaged to be married later in the year. Indeed, life itself seemed to be becoming detached.

My local church provided a ready catalyst for my mixed emotions at this time. The vicar, George, was regarded as an eccentric who did peculiar things, such as trying to push a donkey up the church steps on Palm Sunday. Once, he wanted to knock a big hole in the side of the sixteenth-century tower and turn part of the church into a bookshop-cum-coffee bar. He didn't care a hoot about conservation. 'People matter more than *things*,' was the sentence he repeated like a mantra.

George was a five-point Calvinistic-charismatic-high-Anglican-ritualizing bundle of energy. He had a magnetic personality and the church was packed to capacity every Sunday. The pulpit and brass lectern stood like the fringed ruins of the Acropolis because, as the pews were arranged in a circle, everything happened right in the centre of the church. Healing services regularly took place and when Holy Communion was being celebrated, it was not unusual for the communicants to step over the prostrate bodies of those who had been 'felled by the Spirit'. George had been at it again – laying hands by request on those who felt the need of such ministry. Those who had already been prayed for but had failed to go down were the walking wounded – they stepped over the neutralized bodies as they made their way back to their seats. We did have the exhibitionist characters who staged a mock-comatose state, just above the chancel steps. However, when tea and coffe was about to be served at the back of the church they made a quick recovery.

The place was rich in eccentrics. One old boy regularly

brought his dog to church in a bucket. There was also the lady who presented George with an egg or a fistful of buttons at the communion rail. Con-men, boozy meths-men, prostitutes, all found their way to St Gregory's, and helped to make the church healthily non-institutionalized.

One day George confided to me that he felt it right to go on a sabbatical and study for one year at Fuller Theological Seminary in California. This decision was the result of a recent 'attack' of Church Growth. George, this complex personality, felt he must go and find out more about it. The bishop had given his approval and so, one bright day in the summer of 1977, George flew away to the sunnier climes of California.

The church then went through a series of traumatic changes. A spiky and loveable priest-in-charge was appointed to superintend affairs. I was an elder but couldn't bring myself to revert to a traditional deadpan type of liturgical service that was merely a reflection of my monochrome working life – decent but dead. The dissatis-faction was like a boil that needed squeezing, and George's evangelistic fervour on a cassette tape sent from 6,000 miles away sounded tinny and unconvincing. His enthusiastic accounts of great meetings in Hollywood with dynamic preachers left me feeling like a hiccup in a hur-ricane. I told myself that at fifty-three I wasn't clapped out. God did things with men who were getting on in life. I read the account of Moses' life all over again and became excited when I visualized Caleb's snarl of exasperation when he wanted that mountain (Joshua 14:12).

I had no desire to grow old gracefully and there was no serenity in my spirit. I felt a divine dissatisfaction that continually gnawed at the guts of whatever it was that made me a man. I'd worn blue dungarees for thirty-three years with a desperate dignity. The sights, sounds and smells of the shop floor were becoming ingrained and I carried around like a trademark the distinctive smell of cutting oil in my clothes.

I could not erase the muted misery of long days watching the sun shaft through the skylights of those gaunt Victorian workshops, and the thought of finishing my working life as a crotchety old railway veteran filled me with despair. It was a familiar pattern: all the old boys who were retiring would be carted off to some local village hamlet by a paternal management and a homely pub would euphemistically 'lay on refreshments'. They'd sing a few vintage songs, rehearse some well-turned anecdotes about 'old times' with the usual jokes being trundled out like lame ducks for the fleshpot, and bingo!

I had horrible nightmares of concluding my days as a lollipop man and growing the longest kidney bean on the allotment. Lollipopping and growing long kidney beans are honourable pursuits but I felt I'd got a lot more untapped potential. Too many times I've seen that slightly woebegone look on the face of a sixty-five year old as he makes his lead-footed way around the factory to shake hands with his old mates for the very last time. It's an emotional earthquake for most men. Like old horses destined for the knacker's yard they pad to the factory gate choking back a 'so long' to the security man.

The sheer futility of walking through those gates for the remainder of my working life erupted that January morning when I said, 'I don't want to go to work'.

Of course, I went. Pat and myself got up that morning and went through the usual routine but we both knew that life was going to change. It had to, otherwise my feelings of resentment could quite easily degenerate into bitterness. Even failure in the future was infinitely preferable to wondering what *might* have happened had I taken the plunge and resigned the railway job.

That morning I felt a high sense of relief. I'd done something positive and come to terms with the fact that given the opportunity – not necessarily the ideal one – I'd get out of the rail shops and start again, preferably in another part of the country. In the early years of marriage, with a young family, the sheer economics of such a drastic move would have been potentially disastrous. But now, Pat and me reckoned we'd only one life to live.

Some of my mates must have wondered at my quiet grin of satisfaction that morning. I'd often told them, over the tea-break, that one day I'd get a different job, but nobody really believed me. After all, nobody left the railway after thirty-three years – the paternalistic pull was too strong. *My* father had worked for the industry, *his* father had been a railman and *his* five brothers had all been employed in the railshops. My grandmother's house had been a museum of railwayana. Half a dozen steel pokers, burnished bright, stood on parade in the hearth – illegally manufactured in the works. Sepia photographs of bowler-hatted gaffers strutted across the mantelpiece in front of locos that were once the pride of the Midland Railway Company. Framed mementos of past triumphs in the first aid competitions, proud diplomas for Class 1 marrows in the Open Day Horticultural Show . . . the house depressed me even in my younger days.

Pat was more than willing to share in a future that promised uncertainty and disruption and we reasoned that whatever problems the future might hold, they were problems of life. We had been praying for a more positive ministry and an indication of the next step to take came when, shortly after that momentous January morning, we saw an advert in a religious journal that offered some prospects.

The job itself was not very promising – a property supervisor in a new office complex which a well-known Christian organization had recently taken over. The headquarters were based in one of London's garden suburbs. If I did get the job it would mean we would either have to sell or let our house. We eventually opted for the latter course, having had an indication that a student friend was looking for accommodation.

So, I put pen to paper. Shortly afterwards we received a

charming letter informing us that they'd read some of my articles and books and there was a strong possibility that I might be engaged in some capacity other than a property supervisor. We were invited for an interview.

I went with Pat to meet our prospective employers. We were suitably impressed by the job prospects, and the accommodation provided, and a couple of weeks later we received a letter confirming the appointment and giving a date to start. That evening I wrote out my notice. My hand trembled as I wrote the fateful words consigning my thirty-three years to history. If I had any lingering doubts they evaporated as I thought of all the living-time that lay in the future, being spent in an environment I had grown to hate. Next day I knocked on the door of the boss's office and walked in.

'You look like a man with a message!' he said.

'You're right,' I replied, 'although I don't know whether you're expecting it. I've waited a long time to give you this.' I breathed heavily.

He frowned. 'What do you mean?'

I gave him my notice to quit and he read it slowly.

'You mean you're actually chucking it in – leaving the firm, after all these years? Have you got another job?'

'Yes,' I replied with an edge of one-upmanship. 'I'm going to work in the Smoke.'

'London?' he asked incredulously.

'Yes. I'm moving down there a week on Monday . . . '

The day I actually left the BR workshops was traumatic. I shook hands with my old mates – contemporaries I had known for over thirty years, and their eyes mirrored the futility of all those years spent within the walls of those workshops. I avoided the inquisitional banter of the clock-queue by finishing half an hour early. And then walked out of those gates with the same anonymity as I had walked through them thirty-three years before. There was no parting gift from the management; just one week's wages they owed me, and a buff coloured P45. I never even had a handshake. A friendly nod from the security man on the gate was the final act of the day's proceedings.

When I arrived home I sobbed uncontrollably. All those years had gone, and a terrible feeling of insecurity momentarily rocked the euphoria I had previously felt. Pat laid a reassuring hand on my shoulder. 'We're in it together, love,' she said simply, 'and anyway, we've committed the matter into God's hands so we can face the future with confidence . . . '

The next few days passed very quickly. All the loose ends concerning letting our mortgaged house were tied up and we made the rounds, saying goodbye to all our friends.

Packing my 500 books in strong boxes was a laborious exercise, and Pat was reluctant to leave anything behind she thought might be needed in London. Our sentimental regard for the old and well-loved was felt acutely and packing the furniture in the hire-van the night before we left was an exhausting business. We went to bed tired, a little fearful, feeling like Abraham when he set out for that city whose maker and builder is God, and not really knowing which direction he was to take.

10

A New Start

When we arrived at our destination it was late in the afternoon of the following day. There was a welcoming party of volunteers to help in unloading the van and we were invited into the office for a cup of tea. The person to whom I was immediately responsible in my new role as property manager was a diminutive but business-like lady, an attractive woman in her early forties. While her husband was a remote figure in the upper echelons of the organization, Mrs Lyte ran the day-to-day affairs in the office.

Our first meeting, when I had applied for the job, had been held in an atmosphere of easy informality, but now I detected a different and more alarming note. There was still that polite and engaging concern for our welfare but there was also a certain authoritarianism in her tone. I was soon to learn that her staff of some forty to fifty people had a great regard for her kind and tolerant nature, but at the same time retained a healthy respect for her intellectual capabilities and business acumen. I loved Mrs Lyte at a distance.

The young volunteers who were struggling to carry all our belongings up to our flat on the top floor of the four storey block were a happy bunch. Initially they buckled in with a rare goodwill but the cases of books finally blunted their enthusiasm. By the time they had deposited the last box containing Butler's *Lives of the Saints*, they looked kippered.

The next few hours quickly vaporized. Our eldest daughter, Ruth, with her husband Adrian, and baby,

Matthew Ben, had accompanied us to help us move in, and had spent the night on a makeshift bed made up of a spare mattress on the floor. Because Adrian, a doctor, had to be on duty the following day, they made an early start at 5.30 the next morning. The parting was painful. I felt mentally crippled as I kissed Matthew Ben. It was almost as though part of me was dying and I knew Pat felt the same way. As we watched the van disappear into the grey light of dawn I refused to push my thoughts too far into the future.

I wasn't happy and it wasn't just homesickness, nor a lack of confidence; it seemed to be that uneasy feeling that somewhere along the line we'd misinterpreted the leading of God.

Our new employers had given us leave of absence for the first week to acclimatize ourselves and sort out the curtains and arrange the furniture. I took the opportunity to study the staff as they came into work. Mostly in their early twenties, their faces were serious and there didn't seem much space for that easy levity that somehow lubricated relationships on the shop floor. And yet this *was* a Christian organization. All the ingredients were there – the weekday prayer meeting for the staff, the notice-encrusted corridor full of Praise Nights, Talk-ins, Worship, Drama, Musical Christianaramas . . . Later in the week, as I wandered through the offices I was struck by the intensity of their commitment to the organization. There was an almost frightening dedication that my easy acceptance of life found difficult to come to terms with.

Because work on the complex was not completed, Pat, at a later date, was to take additional work as a cleaner, while I was to start work the week after we arrived. On my first day, Mrs Lyte called me into her office and handed me a slip of paper listing a variety of jobs and numbered one to ten. The first item was: 'Sweep up room where central heating system is installed'.

I made my way to the low prefabricated concrete building. I'd kept my British Rail overalls and they stood out like a sore thumb among the people who worked in the offices. My tools were a large yardbrush with long bristles and a shovel. I set to work with a desperate desire to please.

There was more dust in that place than sand in the desert and soon I was coughing and hacking like a bronchy sailor. But, the job didn't take long, and as I was scooping up the last shovelful Mrs Lyte in her spiky heels clattered up.

'How are things going?' she enquired in a chatty way.

'Not too bad, bit dusty. Not been swept since they built the place,' I replied.

Then Mrs Lyte did something which overturned my thirty years cultivation of Christian grace. She poked her foot under a pipe and kicked out a cigarette-end the workmen had deposited, and which I had failed to sweep up. With a look as though she'd just discovered something nasty under the living room carpet she said, 'You haven't swept under there!'

I suddenly felt a cold anger. I thought of the days I'd shop-stewarded a crowd of men who would have made Moses' Israelites look like a kindergarten school. I thought of my army days, and the time I was lay-pastoring – shepherding my flock on a tough housing estate – and a sense of humiliation began to take control. I turned to her with what I hoped might be a cold and haughty look, but was possibly a snarl.

'Mrs Lyte, this is the first time I've come under matriarchal government and it will be the last. I've swept the dirtiest floors in British Rail workshops and nobody at any time has ever had the audacity to go over my work and say it's not up to standard.'

Her sudden disarming smile knocked me clean off my perch as she said, 'Don't take it so seriously!'

I felt deflated and mumbled inconsequentially, 'I've had a bad night – sorry!' and mentally registered 'one up to the opposition'.

Already I was feeling it was a Them and Us situation and a native inferiority complex was beginning to show. The cultured, well-rounded southern accents of the girls in the office contrasted strongly with my broad Midlands dialect. I felt the odd man out but told myself that it was a Christian organization and I should not feel this resentment and sense of inferiority.

The cultural divide between the shop floor and the antiseptic atmosphere of my new employers also made me uneasy. The four-letter words and general earthiness of my old mates was missing and, strangely, I felt a keen sense of isolation in all this. However, a few days after we had settled in, my role as an accomplished innovator came to the fore.

I usually opened the offices and sorted out the mail in the morning – long before the staff arrived. One particular day I opened up and was confronted by a rat just inside the corridor. It was a fat-bloated rodent – probably pregnant – and its evil eyes balefully regarded me with a malevolent intensity. I reacted quickly and picked up the nearest thing to hand – a fire extinguisher – and threw it, but the rat scuttled behind a door in the corridor, a door which the girls passed by on their way to the upper offices.

I went about my normal duties, occasionally giving the rat a careful glance at a respectful distance. When Mrs Lyte arrived around 8.30 she greeted me with a cosy 'Good morning Ralph, anything to report?'

'Not really,' I replied, 'except there's a Mr Rat to see you'.

She looked puzzled, and evidently misunderstood my jocular remark. 'Rett? I don't think I know a Mr Rett. Where is he?'

'He's sitting eyeing you through that crack in the door, about four feet from the hem of your skirt'.

For a moment the penny didn't drop but then her face became the colour of chalk and she whispered hoarsely, 'A RAT – you're joking of course!'

'No fear. It's the biggest, dirtiest sewer rat I've ever seen in my life. And I've seen a few!'

She began to get a little panicky. 'We must do something,' she wailed. 'The girls will be coming in shortly. What can we do?'

For the first time I felt I'd come into my own. 'Send for the official ratcatcher, a rodent operative. He'll operate under the local authority vermin disposal unit,' I grinned.

She quickly found the telephone number and rang through. They had evidently started work early but were not very helpful, explaining that the ratcatchers had a full schedule and would be dealing with the problem at the earliest opportunity.

'But the rat is behind the door!' screeched Mrs Lyte.

However, the voice at the other end of the phone was equally adamant. 'There is no one to deal with your problem *immediately* . . . ' and with a despairing moan Mrs Lyte put the receiver down and looked at me appealingly.

'Ralph, do you think you could get rid of it . . . ?'

'I suppose I could,' I replied, with just that air of conviction which suggested I disposed of rats every day of my life.

She gasped her gratitude: 'Maybe you could do it while the staff are at prayers?'

The girls eventually arrived – gaggles of demure young ladies, clip-clopping in high heels past the door behind which the rat occupied as his *lebensraum*. I stood smiling my greetings as they trooped up the stairs. Mrs Lyte contained her anxiety and I looked at her with new eyes. She was now very feminine and very vulnerable.

'How are you going to get rid of it?' she asked querulously.

'Have you had a good breakfast?' She looked puzzled, my brand of humour didn't connect.

'Why?' she enquired.

'Forget it! It's nearly time for your prayer meeting – and while you're at your devotions, don't forget your property supervisor and his missus!'

'I shall never be out of your debt! Thank you.'

And she meant it!

So while they were busy at prayer and the place was quiet I prepared to get rid of the rat by fixing a sack between the wall and the door and tipping a heavy book over the top of the door. The rat ran into the sack and I quickly grabbed the neck of the sack and held on tightly. His struggles did not last very long and it was soon despatched to a ratty valhalla by a heavy brick, and buried.

Later in the morning, over coffee in the canteen, Mrs Lyte looked at me and raised her eyebrows and I casually smiled and nodded. But my victory over one rat was only the beginning. They had, it was later discovered, invaded the place, and a man from the vermin removal department arrived to set very large traps in strategic places.

When Pat discovered a bloodied and grotesque, very dead customer in the garbage compound, her revulsion erupted into tears of frustration. Already we had found that the central heating would not turn off, the windows would not open, and the three flights of stairs to our flat became higher every day. The rats added the topstone to her disillusionment.

The garden suburb boasted one high street with a couple of Chinese takeaways, a mini-Woolworths, a collection of nondescript retail shops and a couple of ladies and gents conveniences. After walking up and down a couple of times, we felt we'd exhausted the scenery.

Finally after a month, we decided we'd had enough. Maybe the cultural divide was too great; perhaps we were too old to start a new life in a different part of the country, maybe too set in our ways and unable to adjust to a wholly different life style. Certainly we missed the familiar faces back home. Nobody rang the door bell of our flat, everybody was very polite and kept their distance. I knew Pat was feeling homesick and we both felt hungry to cradle and cuddle Matthew Ben. We missed the matiness of the market traders. There it was impossible to walk through the city centre without meeting someone we knew. Here there was a suffocating respectability; the sense of isolation was acutely felt.

Pat did have some misgivings. Perhaps we hadn't given ourselves enough time to settle in? Again, what would people say when we returned to our home town having fallen flat on our faces? We may have been foolhardy and stupid, but we had begun a new life with such high hopes, firmly believing we had seen the Lord's hand in the matter and convinced we were in the centre of his will. Now, there was only the dull, hollow feeling that, somehow, we had missed out. It seemed God was teaching us in a way that was hard and, at times, incomprehensible.

When we confessed our doubts and frustration to Mrs Lyte we discovered a new facet to her nature. She was a deeply spiritual lady with a highly sympathetic nature and very understanding. We prayed together – Mrs Lyte, Pat and myself – and then came to the bitter decision of when the harsh practicality of the return journey had to be considered.

I put a mayday call through to Mike, one of the elders of the church back home and there was an immediate response.

'We'll hire a van and bring a couple of the lads over next Friday,' he said. 'We'll soon have you back.'

It was with mixed emotions that we worked through our final week. There was a sense of relief that decisive action had been taken and that the future, although uncertain, was to be shaped from a familiar base at home. On the other hand, there was no denying that our journey south seemed to have been a dismal failure . . .

Mike arrived early the following Friday morning with two other stalwarts from church and, once again, we went through the traumatic business of loading the hire van with all our bits and pieces. Our farewells were muted and embarrassing and we were glad to escape from what was potentially a catastrophic situation.

It was a bank holiday weekend when we returned and it seemed every motor vehicle in the British Isles had chosen that particular time to take the north circular route out of London. In two hours we covered just fourteen miles and my brain was fizzing with frustration. I was fed up and sick of the whole venture but managed to put on a brave face for Pat's sake. I suppose she felt the same way but we were saving our post-mortems for later.

Din-deafened and feeling mentally sodden with a heavy diesel smell, we finally reached Derby what seemed umpteen light-years later, albeit much older and wiser.

11

Time on my Hands

Our student friend, Tim, was a teacher and initially he had
rented our house in expectation of staying at least twelve
months. He was most kind and understanding. He had
furnished the place to his own taste but by the time we had
stacked our own furniture the home resembled a furniture
depository. We held a council-of-war and debated the
situation. Although Tim was legally entitled to stay and
exclude us from the house he was very considerate and said
he'd find alternative accommodation as soon as possible.

So we commenced the next stage in our pilgrimage. It
wasn't going to be easy. Tim had his friends and his own
lifestyle. He was a gifted musician and found relaxation in
listening to Beethoven on his hi-fi. My musical appreciation has never gone further than Max Bygraves singing
'You Need Hands', so that long, hot summer promised to
be particularly trying. We discovered areas of our lives that
needed more grace than we had previously imagined.

Pat fortunately got a job as a care assistant in an old
folk's home, but for the first time in my life I was unemployed. I was prepared to eat humble pie and apply for my
old job but the first wave of unemployment was beginning
to bite; all recruitment in BREL workshops had been
stopped. I had presented myself at the local labour
exchange on the first day of my unemployment and
discovered rows of chairs occupied by people in what
seemed to be various stages of mental decay. An air of
stagnant indifference, a peculiar fatalism distinct to
institutionalized-man, hung over the place. It was sad and
depressing.

I marched up to the enquiry desk where a florid-faced woman looked at me, clicked her teeth and said sympathetically, 'If you've got anything else to do duck, go and do it. Come back in an hour.'

After four years in the army, thirty-three years on the shop floor, three years as senior shop steward and twelve years as a lay-pastor, my education was obviously not yet finished. I decided to go and sit in the park and watch the grass grow for an hour. Then I returned to the labour exchange.

A spotty-faced youth with an air of boredom looked at me through pebble-specs.

'I'm unemployed,' I said cheerfully. 'It's my first day!' I knew then that I'd said the wrong thing.

'Gotcha P45?' he asked laconically.

I produced my P45. He then fired a barrage of questions at me but as the glass partition was not a very effective sound conductor, I had difficulty in hearing what he had to say. Industrial deafness is a legacy of the shop floor. I found myself apologizing as he burbled on, viciously stamping various documents.

'Next Monday,' he spelt out as though addressing a backward child, 'go to Becket House in Slade Street at ten o'clock, door C, box four, and sign on. Do-not-neglect-to-do-that! Then ring this number: 4-1-1-1-3, for an appointment with the social security officer for supplementary benefit. Then go to the jobcentre and see what's on offer.'

So, clutching my P45, my UB534 (Leaflet) and my UB40 I left the building feeling fully equipped to join the ranks of the unemployed.

I reported to the jobcentre. It was a joberama place, with flowers spilling out from pots in the walls, little stands with chatty vacancies prominently displayed, and a clutch of clerks decorating the chrome and glass enquiry desk. I was deposited with an earnest young man who took more particulars.

'I don't suppose you have anything in mind?' he asked hopefully.

I summoned up all my resources of Christian charity, gave him a withering grin and said, 'Not really, I'll take anything on offer.'

The young man sent over a few hopeful broadsides. 'There are a few unskilled jobs coming through – it's a question of what appeals to you.'

'I'd like to see the vocational guidance people if possible,' I replied.

The corrugated lines of frustration on his brow relaxed. 'Ah, yes, certainly. Ring this number and fix an appointment.'

When I arrived home I rang the social security people and the jobcentre vocational guidance department.

The DHSS were quick off the mark. At two o'clock next day I found myself sitting in a dilapidated annexe, the walls of which were purposefully notice infested: *Dogs not Allowed; No Smoking; Sit The Other Side Without An Appointment;* and in a KGB atmosphere heavy with anxiety, I waited my turn.

At various intervals a disembodied metallic voice clattered over the tannoy, instructing people to go to numbered cubicles. I waited expectantly for my name to be called. And waited and waited. Eventually I was called. I walked down a long corridor and homed in on box six as requested, to accept the verdict of whoever was to pronounce judgement in my case.

Once again it was a glass-grill encounter. This time my inquisitor was a serious young lady who peered at me through a jazzy pair of spectacles that looked like red hoop-la rings. Particulars were what she wanted. Bank books, mortgage account, deposit accounts, insurance, P45, last wages – you name it, this female fact-finder wanted to know.

The *coup de grâce* was administered with the trained finesse of a matador plunging in the spear: 'You aren't entitled to anything,' she said flatly. 'Come again on the 18th of next month.'

'But I only came in the first place because the labour exchange people advised me,' I croaked. But the interview was over and I lifted myself out of the inquisitorial chair and tottered out of the building.

A week later I went to my appointment at the jobcentre to enquire about some kind of re-training course. Once again my interviewer was a young lady, this time of very ample proportions, who lolled in her chair reading the form I had filled in. I remembered the form:

Question	What would you like to do given a free choice?
Answer	Be a lighthouse keeper, antiquarian bookseller, television reviewer.
Question	How have you changed in the last ten years?.
Answer	For the better. Wiser, more handsome, tolerant, kinder.
Question	What are your most pleasing/unpleasing characteristics?

After I had screwed up my face, trying to look mean and nasty and, alternatively, Christianly good and kind, I gave up and did not answer.

I had filled in that form with a zealous disregard for what effect it might have on my future. It seemed the only pre-emptive strike I could make against bureaucracy. I could not sit idly by.

I was promised that by the end of the interview, which would last up to an hour and a half, I would be better equipped to know where my future might lie. She began her spiel. What were my expectations? Job inclinations? I told her I wanted to do something academic – maybe a librarian? I had read somewhere how older men could be re-trained not only as paviors, painters and plasterers but also as social workers, probation officers and suchlike.

After some skirmishing in the no-man's land of verbal

communication she gave me one of those sad-sack smiles, all sympathy and saccharine, and gave her considered judgement. At fifty-three I was – dare she say it – too old. Job prospects after re-training were slim. Being fifty-three I had nerved myself for this crisis and I was less bothered than she appeared to be. I took my twelve and a half stone of saleable labour out of the building.

I applied for a variety of jobs including a commissionaire at a local brewery. This experience was an eye-opener. I first had to become a member of the Corps of Commissionaires and as an ex-serviceman I was eligible, so I went to Birmingham to be registered. Having been accepted I then went for the job interview. There were two of us, my rival being a beery-faced, fat little man who seemed to have difficulty in breathing. He told me he was sixty-two years old and had applied unsuccessfully for twenty-odd jobs. I sympathized but felt sure this would be his twenty-first failure. With my best charcoal-grey smile to fit my charcoal-grey suit I reeled off my curriculum vitae to a young bloke, sizzling with efficiency. I felt I had to match the mood of the moment. When I got home I told Pat it was 'in the bag' and I'd soon be directing VIPs to other VIPs and shunting visitors to their respective locations.

Five days later I received a letter informing me that I had been unsuccessful. I subsequently discovered that the fat little bloke with the crumpled face had got the job. Pride goes before a fall and that was one lesson which was particularly wounding to my self-esteem.

At home I was experiencing a reversal of the roles. Pat was now the breadwinner and my working-class values took a further knock. A kind of mental torpor followed and I felt like a clock that needed winding up; a sensation of uselessness and rejection began to burn inside me, fuelled by the dreadful boredom of long sunny afternoons with a load of potential and no buyers.

I took refuge in the past, re-read old diaries, looked at

sepia photographs of my soldiering days when I had a sense of destiny and a cause to fight for. It was all so totally artifical, negative and self-defeating. I was clapped out, over the hill; time was not an ally and I had reached the point of no return.

It was the part that nobody saw that hurt most. I had been taken out of circulation and it had not made the slightest difference to society. I was another cipher in a politician's speech, another statistic. Even some church folk looked embarrassed when I told them I was out of work.

The three months I was unemployed was one long bereavement. The point was, not only was I the corpse but I was also the chief mourner. God knows how people cope with an extended period of unemployment. I only know that for me it had a debilitating, corrosive effect.

I certainly missed the camaraderie of the shop floor and it became increasingly more difficult to maintain a disciplined structure to my life. Before I left the railway, Saturday had always been regarded as the end of the working week – an extra lie-in, a visit to the local library, a civilized breakfast. But now, every day seemed the same. I adopted the practice of putting on my tie and polishing my shoes to go to the library. Changing my library books became an Event.

I saw many of my dole-queue mates in town and although I felt a ghetto mentality was something to avoid, it was comforting to share a common experience with those who were familiar with dole-queue blues. There were other times when I felt unjustifiably ashamed and guilty when strangers asked me what I did for a living. The Protestant Work Ethic dies hard. We still assess the worth of a person by what kind of work he is paid to do.

It would have been easy to throw in the towel and have an impersonal giro cheque dropped through the letter box, but looking back I can see God's hand in the experience. He sometimes has to allow us to be put on the anvil and

90

from there, smash us back into shape. For me, being unemployed was, in some ways, a therapeutic process. The real problems I encountered were the withdrawal symptoms.

I had at least gained something very precious – liberation from the factory floor. I had proved to myself that it *was* possible to assert human dignity above the demands of a shackled spirit, and I still believed that God had a purpose in what seemed like failure and defeat.

We had taken up the threads at our old church but the departure of its mercurial and charismatic vicar to America had caused great fissures in the fellowship. There was a natural grouping of middle class leadership which plotted the future direction of the church.

George's departure had caused a vacuum which was predictably filled by those whose function by tradition it was to lead. His vision of a body of elders chosen because of their leadership potential rather than their social class was becoming a non-starter.

The priest in charge found difficulty in coping with pockets of anti-Anglicanism. All shades of Christian affiliation were represented – the healers, the fringe groups with a particular emphasis on deliverance and exorcism, whole-food-care-of-the-earthers, Christian socialists, anti-nukers, liberation theologiamaniacs, total sanctificationists... it was a church on the boil. Of course, there was a strong caucus of orthodox, committed evangelicals who somehow gave coherence to the strange amalgam.

Even with George's departure, it was a church which attracted a large congregation drawn from the whole social spectrum and there were some quite remarkable conversions and miraculous healings. Although there had been a subtle alteration in the style of leadership, the momentum that George had started was being maintained. But at this point I felt I had run out of steam.

The zipped-up singing and emotive preaching, the input of so many amorphous groups was too much to cope with.

I adopted a low profile and with Sunday evening free, Pat and I started attending a small nonconformist church which was calmer and more balanced in its worship. In tandem, this arrangement suited us. On Sunday mornings we fastened our seat belts and were borne along by the sheer unpredictability of Corinthian-like excitement, where everything was happening at once – a church with problems of life. In the evening, we relaxed in a sandwich service that probably topped-up our spiritual batteries. So life went on . . .

Coming out of the public library one day I happened to see a traffic warden. He was standing on a busy street corner, dressed in his smart uniform, his arms folded and the autumnal sun burnishing his buttons. The thought suddenly struck me that his was a job I'd like to do. I have never been a motorist and did not realize the antipathy of motorists towards traffic wardens. Later it became painfully obvious. I innocently thought the bloke with a yellow band round his hat was a mobile No Parking sign. I went up to him.

'Excuse me,' I said, 'are there any jobs going in your department?'

'I think there might be one vacancy,' he replied in clipped officialese, 'and for that I would advise you to apply at the central police station.'

It was the fastest move in animal creation. I presented myself to the granite-faced policewoman behind the enquiry desk and breathlessly enquired if they wanted any traffic wardens. She looked at me sympathetically and handed me a form.

'There might be a vacancy,' she replied in a non-committal sort of waymode of speech that I was later to become very familiar with. 'Fill in this form and return it as soon as possible.'

My heart was light and I was tremendously excited. When Pat came home later that night I told her I might get a job as a traffic warden.

'Don't forget the commissionaire episode,' she said, laughing. 'I don't think you do very well applying for jobs where you have to wear a uniform.'

'I wore a boiler suit for thirty-three years,' I replied, 'and don't tell me *that's* not a uniform!'

When the letter arrived inviting me for an interview I was much more restrained and we prayed over this application. When the great day arrived, the police inspector put me at my ease and I was relaxed and happy with his questions.

'A traffic warden's job isn't to book as many motorists as he can,' he said. 'It's his job to keep the streets free from parked vehicles in restricted areas. We are here to serve the public.'

I nodded and thought about the warden I had seen standing enjoying the scenery in the morning sunshine. I might be able to serve the public for years if it involved a good deal of *that*.

A few days later I received a letter telling me I had got the job subject to a satisfactory medical report and within a few weeks I was installed as Traffic Warden 97.

12

On the Beat

I spent the first three weeks of my new job in the company of a trained colleague and was initiated into the art of 'knocking off' illegally parked cars. I had not yet been measured for my uniform and my cloth cap, reefer jacket and hush puppies hardly seemed to project the right image, even for a trainee. Oblique comments from shopkeepers on my beat were met by my assurance that the civvy clothes did not represent a secret surveillance unit of the traffic warden service. The days were getting cooler and I welcomed the introductions to kindly shopkeepers who invited us in for a cuppa. I remembered seeing an advertisement which said, *Do you want an open-air job? Do you like meeting people? Then why not consider becoming a traffic warden?* The bit about an open-air job lodged in my memory after I had weathered a series of force 8 winds and rain!

The Official Secrets Act which I was obliged to sign effectively scotched any idea I might have had about making a living by giving the *News of the World* an unexpurgated account of the darker side of traffic wardening. And my official notebook was also meticulously signed and certified, ensuring that the 100 pages were correctly numbered. But the day I was issued with my uniform is most indelibly etched in my memory. When I looked in a full length mirror I thought I was a reflection of somebody who had escaped from an amateur dramatic production of *The Desert Song,* or an early Ealing comedy. Maybe I wouldn't have looked such a smart advert ,for the brewery after all.

I was employed at a police station located in a run-down area of the city. The place was built like a fortress and designed to withstand a siege. TV surveillance cameras, automatic doors and stony-faced plain clothed coppers all created the impression that Big Brother was on the door-step.

There was a large immigrant community in the vicinity, with a variety of shops displaying everything from exotic Eastern spices to mysteriously worded Asiatic banking concerns, thus ensuring a continual flow of traffic through the streets. My beat also ran through the city's red-light ground, half a dozen mosques, a variety of churches, Chinese take-aways and second-hand car dealers. It was altogether a fascinating district – rich in sights, sounds and smells.

My colleagues were also varied: a couple of ladies, divorcees, with a deadly serious approach to keeping the streets tidy of offending motor vehicles as a way of life. Then there was Katy, an attractive frothy haired blonde with blue eyes. She gave out parking tickets with a giggle to male motorists who positively enjoyed the booking. My male colleague was sad-sack Charlie, an ex-soldier who lived in his memories and to whom life was one long funeral. He would solemnly return the salute of ageing Indian gentlemen who, with memories of the Raj, respected his medal ribbons. Charlie was never known to smile, not even on the rare occasions he discovered a stolen car on his beat.

The two gaffers, senior wardens, were matey people who looked after the gaggle of wardens with a paternal regard for their welfare: 'If that Vauxhall says *that* again Cindy, after you've warned him, tell me and I'll tell Inspector Brain and we'll have a copper knocking on his door!'

It was a job of confrontations, form filling and bureaucratic bumbledom. I must have got through a couple of processed Canadian pine forests with all the paperwork I encountered. It was also a valuable seed bed for the budding pastor. All life was on the streets. The humour, the pathos, the weaknesses and strengths all were encountered in the job. And my uniform became a lightning conductor for all the static in the human heart.

I was regularly called upon to sort out the problem of dead cats messing up the road and frightening the children after being run over. Dear old ladies would stop me and ask if I could fix their tellys and wonky broom handles. As a direction-finder I was pretty useless but I did my best: juggernaut lorries would be directed to the ring road no matter what their destination might have been. I worked on the assumption that after circling the city half a dozen times the drivers would get fed up and ask somebody else.

I regularly stood beside an illegally parked car and waited the customary ten minutes before booking the driver. I would often remove my cap and sincerely pray that the offender would return before I did the deed. Although there was no explicit instruction that so many parking tickets should be issued, there was a tacit understanding that one could not be doing the job effectively without *some* statutory fines being imposed. And that was my area of difficulty. My pocket book was full of 'warnings' with few actual bookings.

On one occasion when I was feeling the pressure of my negative response over a long period, I saw a car parked where it should not have been in a quiet street. I watched it for a quarter of an hour and then attached a parking ticket to the windscreen. On this occasion, I didn't pray so I suppose divine intervention was thwarted. A few weeks later I was on the beat and saw my local vicar, a much-loved but harassed man who confessed to me that 'he'd like my job'. I murmured something about the pain and the problems but he said I was more than compensated by the freedom to move around and shut off at the end of the day.

He then said conversationally, 'You know Ralph, for the first time in over forty years motoring I fell foul of the law not so long ago.' I was more than interested as he continued, 'I parked my car in John Street – I was taking communion to a ninety year old lady, blind and house-bound – and when I returned, I found a parking ticket on the windscreen.'

I felt distinctly uneasy. 'John Street', I croaked opening my pocket book, 'around 10.30 on the morning of the 5th March?'

'That's it,' and he gave me one of those loving, sympathetic looks as the penny dropped. 'Ah, *you* booked me. Don't worry Ralph, no hard feelings. After all, it's your job!'

I told him to write to headquarters explaining the circumstances and he'd be let off. He hadn't paid the fine yet and so I was able to put a report in to my superiors asking for leniency in this particular case. I couldn't have booked a nicer bloke. I ought to have prayed.

Traffic wardening modified my outlook on those folk who wear Jesus stickers, fishes, doves, crosses and Bibles in their buttonholes. All those bits of ironmongery that serve to tell out the good news can be potentially damaging to the cause they promote. They are an inevitable challenge to the world around and if the badgewearer's character matches up to the little lapel cross – praise God! – but if the wearer suffers from periodic bouts of amnesia about their Christian affiliation, then all the Church is clobbered.

I recall an incident where a motorist seemed to be having difficulty in starting his car so I politely asked if I could help – maybe he wanted a push . . . ? He snorted and looked at me with a pair of snarling eyes doing a sabre dance. He didn't even acknowledge the offer of assistance. Perhaps he felt under the weather. Anyway, all at once he started the car, did a Starsky and Hutch U-turn and roared away. I just caught a glimpse of a prominent sticker in the rear window which assured the world at large (and traffic wardens in particular) *Jesus Loves You*. Now, that is a highly loaded statement which, if time and opportunity had permitted, I would like to have pursued further with that particular driver. Honking his testimony in the back of the car could have seriously complicated things.

Still, I'm glad it was *me* he was sore with. I might have had a hard time explaining to my colleagues that even Christians are human and sometimes get fed up with traffic wardens.

13

A Change of Uniform

Wearing a traffic warden uniform was a preparation for the day I'd be wearing a dog collar. Both acted as a brake on my more tempestuous nature. When an irate motorist – legitimately booked for a parking offence – lost his temper and made heated allegations regarding my parents and pedigree I could never allow my feelings to get the upper hand. I always had to be mindful of what the uniform represented and suffocate a natural tendency to indulge in verbal pyrotechnics.

There are whole areas of concern in the Christian's prayer life – the dispossessed, hungry, bereaved, homeless – but we rarely remember those who perform the necessary but unpopular jobs at the rump end of our complex society. During my time as a traffic warden I met people professionally when they were vulnerable, sensitive and very often emotionally upset at being discovered transgressing the law. Any job which involves a Christian in relationships at that level, of necessity, brings in God's involvement. It wasn't difficult to theologize my job.

Many Christians actually believed that one could not be a Christian *and* a traffic warden. Some felt it was a 'bad testimony' and being a traffic warden did for Christianity what the charge of the Light Brigade did for recruitment in the Crimean War. But I was never able to enforce the law without recognizing that in the final analysis, God is the lawgiver and unless God was alongside me on the streets, feeling the pain of rejection and the angry snarls of folk caught offending the parking laws, then my Sunday worship was invalid and meaningless.

Particularly in the multi-racial areas, the rich variety of sights, sounds and smells was always a diversion from the obvious business at hand. Yet some of the sights would have caused the angels in heaven to gently lay down their harps and weep. The sounds – mainly in the predominantly 'Little Delhi' sector of the city – sounded to my untutored Western ears like a regiment of mentally deranged bagpipe players. And, at their extremes, the smells alternated between the delicious tang of strong curry and a bleach-scoured urinal.

I often passed locked and barred Victorian churches – mainly on street corners – looking like decaying sarcophagi or crumbling monuments to a long-since dead cultic religion. But on the streets there was light and life and movement, and God was evident in his own creation. It was Studdert Kennedy who said he saw more evidence of God in a lamp post than in a star – man made the lamp post to give him light. On the streets I saw the truth that when God speaks there is action, and the daily activity of social man, man being the acme of God's created order, was the evidence that God was at work.

Law enforcement at any level is an indication that human society is inherently sinful. Wearing a traffic warden uniform was, for me, a manifestation of society's desire to conform to that state which enables man to live a civilized existence. I recognized that this necessarily involved some degree of pain both on the part of the law enforcer and the law breaker. God always spoke in that moment when there was a verbal backlash, after a courteous approach to an offending motorist. It was, for me, an extension of the cross. The Holy Communion and the honking cars had a connection, and it was this aspect of rejection that made me keenly aware of the presence of God in my daily occupation. It was more than merely traffic wardening; the whole meaning of Christ's redemptive work was crystallized in that distinctive attitude of complete and utter contempt on the part of a large section

100

of the public to a bloke in uniform, genuinely trying to do the job society had decreed that *somebody* should do.

One's sensitivity as a Christian sharpened when it was categorically stated as an article of working practice that at no time was it permissible to say, 'I'm sorry' to a member of the public. To admit the possibility of error was to undermine the majesty of the law. Such an admission on the part of the traffic warden was out of the question, and yet a whole army of scriptural injunctions concerning the fallibility of fallen man made me aware of the brittle nature of his attempt to live according to the highest and the best. My traffic warden days were an exposition of Romans 7, always trying but always making a hash-up, beginning each day with the noble intent not to book any cars but then the moral dilemma that I was being paid to do just that.

There came a time when God spoke to me through the eyes of the meths men and the junkies, the prostitutes and petty thieves – all those who formed part of the sub-culture where I worked my patch. The unutterable sadness of lives ravaged by sin, fragmented lives, unwholesome and dirty. Sometimes the harvest field where we are called to go is mucky and we need to wear our working boots.

I recall seeing a lad of about seventeen years old in a shop doorway, bent double in agonizing pain. He had venereal disease in an advanced stage and was afraid to tell anyone. Then there was the fifteen year old prostitute with a forty year old look in her eyes. I cultivated the friendship of a young policeman seconded to the vice squad who confessed he was spiritually and mentally scarred by the pornography he was exposed to. All these experiences were bound up in my job and were part of the totality of my life. The conflict between good and evil, God and Satan, was not abstract but actual.

But it was not all murky and overloaded with theological imponderables. A rewarding aspect involved children. I was often admired by the Indian boys and girls – my uniform displayed a certain dignity and authority.

'Hello' they'd shout. 'Are you a policeman?'

'Not quite!' I'd smirk but then they would run after me shouting 'Hello! hello!' After I had reciprocated in like manner fifty times my bottom jaw began to sag. But the kids enjoyed it. They had none of the biting cynicism and suspicion of their elders.

It was always a welcome break to be put on the school crossing patrol when the lollipop lady couldn't make it and I always found it easy to talk to the children about Jesus. They brought me their many problems.

'How did I *know* there were no traffic wardens in heaven?'

That was easy, 'Because boys and girls play in the streets' (Zechariah 8:5).

'What's heaven like?'

'For a start, they put gold in banks down here, but in heaven they use the precious stuff as paving stones and walk on it!'

There was a happy innocence and burbling joy about the children as they ran up to me to be shepherded across the busy road. And God was in all this activity.

It was always music to my ears to pass a playground and hear the happy sounds of laughter and shouting, the dancing and gaiety, the games of rounders and hopscotch. It seemed to me to be a true picture of the shalom of God, the beauty of holiness without the cultic trappings. Yet if this were *only* a picture, the reality must be even more wonderful!

The mind of a child is direct. The questions it asks are genuine and pointed. And the uniform gave an imprimatur to each answer. When one of the children asked, 'How *can* God speak to us?' I would reply, 'God speaks to us through mums and dads, dogs, rain, telly, books – a million ways but chiefly he talks to us through Jesus. And he fills up the holes in heaven with stars so we can take a peep at the shininess of heaven!'

I suppose the child psychologist would gloomily forecast brain-corrosion at an early age and the academic theologian would consider the answer completely crackpot, but it was all part of the fun of discovering God!

In the light of Romans 13 the role of my job took on another perspective. Civil government and law enforcement officers are promoted by God and if they are seen to be doing a good and necessary job, must be supported. In these days of rebellion against authority it is also good to remind ourselves that the structures of human government are not founded on God's arbitrary will but on the needs of humanity to secure the highest good.

The purpose of the Christian in any occupation is to reflect the concern of God for his people. All work is a calling from God and a service to him and our fellow men and women and Christians are ministers of his purpose. Christian traffic wardens, like Christian parsons or Christian plumbers, are in the business of ministering shalom and there can be no distinction between the secular and the sacred.

It was a bright autumnal morning. I had been a traffic warden for about a year and it was beginning to show. I had a hunted look in my eyes on football match days when the crowds had fun at my expense. But on this particular morning my responsibilities were more amenable. The Gas Board were digging a large hole in the middle of the road and my job was to keep the traffic moving. I merely had to watch the space between the hole and the pavements. Pat would regularly have a chat with me on her shopping rounds and on this day she had news.

'Guess what,' she said excitedly, 'George is returning next month.' I nearly fell in the hole as she went on, 'We had a letter this morning – he's looking forward to coming back.'

It was indeed a heartening piece of news. The promise of another spiritual springtime was in the air. I had never lost faith that one day I would find my true vocation, but it seemed that for a long time my life had been like a barge moving upstream; the journey had often been static, I spent a lot of time waiting for the lockgates to open.

The first service George conducted on his return lacked the usual élan. Maybe the fault lay in us. Much had happened since the day he left to go to the States. We had been through many different experiences and had learnt that God's strategy in developing character didn't necessarily run in straight lines. George had also changed. There was a note of subdued pessimism in his preaching. Later he was to tell me that his long-term vision for St Gregory's had foundered and he had plateaued in his ministry. He had taken the people as far as he possibly could and was praying seriously about moving.

We were chatting in his study one day when casually he said, 'Have you ever thought about offering yourself for the ministry?'

'You mean the Church of England?'

'Yes', he replied. 'We need people who haven't been through the system – folk like yourself whose college has been life, experience on the shop floor.'

I felt a bit like Moses and volunteered a dozen reasons why I could never measure up to the demands. I'd left school at the outbreak of the Second World War when I was just thirteen years old, had a series of dead-end jobs before joining the army at seventeen. I'd been de-mobbed at twenty-two and having no skills or qualifications of any kind, felt I hadn't much to offer.

'But you've educated yourself,' persisted George, 'and there's no reason why at least you shouldn't test the water.'

Pat and I went away and prayed for guidance. We spoke to Christian friends and eventually, I decided to talk to my bishop – a man who I trusted and whose judgement I respected. He was sympathetic and suggested I go ahead with the initial moves. After the local selection procedure, I was invited to go before ACCM (the Advisory Council for the Church's Ministry).

I was quite open about my plans at the police station and although my colleagues thought it rather odd that a traffic warden should consider being a Church of England cleric, they were quite enthusiastic. It was about this time that the BBC decided to use a script I had submitted, so when a camera team descended on the police station it was with some panache that the traffic wardens hoofed their beats. They always had a sense of inferiority compared with the police who had powers of arrest. Indeed, all kinds of legal muscle were at *their* disposal in an emergency but the poor old traffic warden had to rely on his campaign ribbons – if he had any. So my colleagues basked in the light of the TV cameras and enjoyed the one-upmanship.

I was very conscious of my inadequacies when I took the train up north for the ACCM three day residential selection conference. I had few doubts in my mind that I would be rejected. The bishop and I had talked together about the area of ministry where I felt a vocational call – industrial chaplaincy – but parallel with this was the whole process of training following orthodox lines at a theological college.

As it happened, I soon realized that the selection conference – whatever the outcome – was an unqualified success from my point of view. It was a time of discovery. I made new friends and thoroughly enjoyed the fellowship and spiritual input. The interviewing sessions were not as daunting as I had anticipated. There was friendly discussion about my areas of strength and weakness and a good deal of sympathetic understanding about my non-academic background.

The enormity of the decision I had taken dawned on me at Compline on the very first night. It was late and somewhat reluctantly I had made what I regarded as an almost obligatory appearance at this service. I had always regarded Compline as a faint whiff of spiky Anglo-Catholicism, to be avoided unless absolutely necessary. It was pure prejudice because I hadn't the faintest idea what Compline was all about. Anything savouring of monasticism was an anathema and my evangelical background reacted against this imposition. But, feeling under some moral pressure, I went.

Eighteen aspiring ordinands from widely differing backgrounds sat in the tiny chapel with five minutes to go before the start of the service. I have always found silence difficult to cope with. I am conscious of my body, my breathing, my thoughts and surroundings and too much silence creates a certain tension in my mind. This, coupled with the thought that I was probably being assessed even as I sat there made me feel most miserable so I was relieved when the elderly priest commenced the service. I had a shock. It wasn't a bit like I expected – that dead formality which cripples the human spirit and makes a mockery of a living faith. True, we had a liturgical pattern but then the old boy perched himself on a chair in the nave and conversationally spoke to us about the call of God. I fail to recall much of what he had to say but there was a point where he half-humorously contrasted the values of the world with the riches of the Christian faith and he finished up saying, 'You don't get much in the way of material rewards as a priest.' Then he paused, smiled, and dismissed the world with, 'But you get enough.'

Maybe if he had concluded on a profoundly moving note of spiritual clarity where perhaps the angels and choirs of heaven were singing paeans of praise in my head I might have forgotten that service, but God spoke to me in the *simplicity* of the hour; there was a horizontal authenticity which struck a chord. I knew I had reached a critical point in my spiritual pilgrimage and felt the impetus of God's guidance in a very real way – almost a replay of 'This is the way, walk in it' (Isaiah 30:21).

On the morning of my departure from the selection conference I felt an inner serenity that, whatever the outcome, I had done the right thing in offering myself for ordination . . . the future I could leave in God's sure hands.

14

The Meaning of Ministry

Parallel with the lengthy ACCM selection procedure I had
sought an interview at St John's Theological College in
Nottingham. I had been advised that available places were
rapidly filled and if I *was* selected for training I might have
difficulty in obtaining a college place unless I applied fairly
early.

I had already been for a preliminary interview in Nottingham and Pat, of course, accompanied me. Our future
was inextricably bound up together and any dramatic
change in my circumstances would inevitably affect her.

Sitting on the bus, returning from the ACCM selection
conference, I remembered the interview at St John's. It was
another exercise in the art of serendipity. Me and Pat had
sat in a book-lined study balancing cups of coffee and
munching arrowroot biscuits. I had felt a certain disorien-
tation, as though my past was trying to catch up on me.
The railway days seemed a long way off. The unhappy
London experience, unemployment and knocking off cars
contrasted sharply with these halls of academe. The
college staff member who conducted the interview seemed
to me an oddity compared to the people I had met and
worked with. When I gently asked him if he had ever
worked with ordinary folk he gave me a cherubic smile and
said, 'Why of course! I often have to go to Oxford and talk
to the college people there.' His answer gave me cause for
reflection. There was an other-worldly atmosphere about
the place, everywhere seemed socially sanitized. I noticed
that everyone was super-polite. The oleaginous introductions to other members of staff and students as we were

shown round the college reinforced my conviction that I would have to re-jig my thinking to accommodate the college outlook.

Being a geriatric fifty-three year old necessitated some modification in the college syllabus and subject to being accepted by ACCM it was decided that I should do the essay course normally arranged for mature students and running over two years. In my case I would do a concentrated one year course of study which involved writing sixteen essays. There was also a one year placement in a local church and it was stressed that this would be totally different in churchmanship from my home church where I had ministered with George.

So the spadework was done and, provided the selectors were satisfied with my suitability for training, I thought I had a broad idea of what was expected of me.

Two weeks after returning from my ACCM, a letter arrived from the bishop expressing his delight that I had been accepted for training. I wasn't as elated as I thought I might have been. The full-time ministry had always seemed an awesome vocation and I was very scared about the future.

On the day of my departure from the traffic warden service there was a good deal of leg-pulling regarding my inability to remember car numbers and parking regulations. But the wardens were a good bunch of people and there were cream cakes all round as I was presented with a Parker pen and a reminder that if I became a priest, 'send up one or two prayers for the traffic wardens'.

I felt a certain cultural inferiority about taking up orders in the established Church. Indeed, I had felt quite diminished at St John's . . . But Pat and I reasoned that having asked God for guidance we would move within the perimeter of a great assurance. Financially some sacrifice was involved but this had been anticipated and such funding as the *Church Times* Train-a-priest fund and the Church Pastoral-Aid Society provided, subsequently helped us through the lean period.

On the morning of 28 September 1981 I arrived at St John's College to commence my training. Once again I was transported by Adrian, my son-in-law, in his faithful but battered Beetle.

I had gained the impression in my initial interview that St John's was like an orbiting space-lab where everything needed for survival was on board so my personal survival kit included a copy of O. Henry's short stories, a double album cassette of Max Bygrave's *100 Singalong Songs* and a thesaurus in dictionary form. I had also strapped my bike onto the roof rack so I reasoned I had something for my body, mind and spirit.

The manicured lawns with regimented rows of bushes and shrubs never looked greener and more respectable. We pulled into the drive. Matthew Ben decided to do an initial survey so he wobbled to the nearest rhododendron bush and began to dissect the heads. I split the refined atmosphere by hollering my disapproval and Matthew took the hint and began to bawl his eyes out. It was all good fun. I obtained the keys to my room and Adrian gave me a hand to convey my belongings.

I spent the first day familiarizing myself with my new surroundings and greeting my fellow students. Some were returning after a long summer break, others were like myself – new boys – although I suppose I was the greenest of the bunch having only a hazy idea of what to expect.

It didn't take long to settle in and I discovered a number of men on my corridor who were married with small children. They were making quite considerable sacrifices in training for the ministry. Quite a few had held lucrative jobs in industry when they had responded to the call to ordination. My personal view was – and is – that the wives should also stand up, with their menfolk, during the ordination service. Coping with small children and running a home with a husband away at college demands a very high degree of commitment. Relatively, I was giving up very little and just sixteen miles separated me from Pat.

Bryan, an ex-teacher who was billeted in the next 'cell' to mine, was a skilled practitioner in the art of brewing beer. Arthur, the corridor 'card', had worked on merchant ships and had a taste for the high life. It was only a taste however and the residue of his affluent lifestyle before he entered the college was carried over in his Mercedes, telly and expensive hi-fi. Gregory was the corridor warden, a kind of sanctified shop steward who took his job very seriously – he sorted out involved problems such as why C corridor only had one small brown loaf allotted, and who might have pinched the vacuum cleaner. Besides organizing the weekly corridor prayer-meeting he was a general factotum, an all-purpose dogsbody, an Aunt Sally bring-your-troubles-to-Zilla kind of man. The theologiamaniacs on C corridor kept him fully occupied.

A stimulating crowd of people – I was certainly going to enjoy the community atmosphere, but the academic input I looked upon with trepidation. Sure enough, the first two weeks were harrowing and my ignorance, even of basic essentials, was very evident. When titles for conducting seminars were put 'on offer', the other students were looking down the list and indicating their preferences but I hadn't the foggiest idea what a seminar was. It could have been the female gender of a semibreve on a tonalscale. I was left with the last title which proved to be some obscure dissertation on the *filioque* clause. However, I discovered I had a native ability to grasp the main thread of a theological argument. The fact that some of the theology was erudite, obscure or totally incomprehensible I put down not to the content but the rotten craftsmanship of the authors. As R.C. Zaehner, Spalding Professor of Eastern Religions and Ethics at Oxford wrote in reference to modern liberal Protestants, 'The dear theologians whose quantitive output continues to be prodigious but whom nobody ever reads except theology students (they have to) and the theologians themselves who have to keep abreast of the

110

latest theological fashion because that apparently, is what they are paid to do.' On the whole, theologians are bad communicators. William Barclay paid a high price for his ability to translate theology in terms the common man understood – he was never recognized as an academic theologian of any stature by his contemporaries.

When I eventually discovered what was required of me by my mentors at St John's, I was happy. I knew I had the ability to master the course. It was not so with a number of my fellow students. One chap in particular, a university graduate, came to me one evening with tears in his eyes.

'It's no good Ralph,' he said, 'I'll never get through. I just can't write *essays*.'

'But you've been through university,' I replied. 'You've got a degree!'

'But that's in my chosen subject. We didn't have to write essays – it was mostly drawings and diagrams. Can you help me?'

And of course, I did, as I helped a number of other highly qualified people. I used to joke that 1,500 words on Amos would cost them a fiver but an essay titled, 'Is Conscience a Bad Joke Played on Us by Divine Providence?' would be ten quid. Even so, I always found the marking system of the papers rather odd because a suitably 'laundered' Bultmann only registered about 58 per cent and I reasoned that if *he* couldn't make at least 75 per cent there was no hope for the rest of us.

I soon adjusted to college routine. It was particularly satsifying that for the first time in fifty-odd years I was trusted to do things without a gaffer at my elbow. Skiving from tutorials, lectures and mandatory services wasn't in my book. I never had any difficulty in early rising but some of the students appeared at tutorials with their brains undressed and confided how much they welcomed a time of 'quiet meditation' when they might close their eyes and drift into a state of narcophilia without feeling conspicious.

My strong fundamentalist convictions took a battering from the liberal theology that was freely ventilated in the lectures and debates (although I suspect that a certain deliberate provocation was healthy for stimulating reflection and asking pertinent questions). In the give and take of the seminars I was at liberty to take a few pot-shots at the modish figures who inspired a certain awe in the minds of the staff. I thought Canaan Banana was an invention of Peter Simple of the *Daily Telegraph's* 'By the Way' column, and wrote a satirical article about him in the college magazine – one of the lecturers rebuked me sharply. All those theologians with boom-sounding Teutonic names . . . Schleiermacher, Bultmann and Bonhoeffer . . . with their wordy wildernesses which very few of us understood seemed to me to have little relevance to life as it is lived. As an academic exercise for professional theologians I suppose they had a place, but I tended towards William Temple's description of this particular breed: 'Men who spend blameless lives by giving entirely orthodox answers to questions no one is asking'.

I once told the Old Testament lecturer (a man I admired and respected even though I thought him a heretic) that one day in heaven, he'd put his arm around my shoulder and say, 'You were right all along, Ralph'. I could never envisage walking down Celestial Boulevard in heaven and being introduced to Isaiah, and not being sure whether he was Isaiah 1, 2 or 3.

Life on the corridor was at times reminiscent of my army days when we were bonded together by strong ties of fellow-feeling and comradeship. We laughed together, wept together and learnt a great deal about the *koinonia*.

I was always assured of a lift home at weekends to see Pat, when I took the opportunity to attend to things that needed attention in the home. Pat was coping tremendously well. Her job as a care assistant in the old people's home absorbed most of her time and Ruth and Adrian did not live too far away. It was good to see Matthew Ben making steady progress and I looked forward to my 'parole' at weekends. The college was another world; I needed to be 'earthed' with what I called 'real people'.

My placement church situated in a dormitory village and to which I was attached on Sundays was also a growth point. It accommodated a predominantly, though not exclusively, young, middle class grouping of business folk who commuted the short distance into the city. The mock Georgian houses in this mini Virginia Water complemented rather than competed with the rural setting, although there were times when I felt that it had a quality of unreality.

'There used to be ten farms here but now there's only one,' was the comment of the churchwarden. Judging by the pungent animal-smells which occasionally permeated the village, the authenticity of its farming origins was hard to deny. Nevertheless, I got the impression that it was a tight little, right little enclave of middle-class solidarity; a formidable redoubt against the stealthy encroachment of late twentieth century technology and its Great Levelling process. A green belt effectively cushioned the well-heeled villagers from the developers and neatly insulated them from a council estate that spawned certain fears in the hearts of the older inhabitants.

The aggressive solidarity of the community was no more exemplified than when the city council proposed itinerant caravan dwellers be allocated a permanent site half a mile from St Wystan's, the village church. An action committee was instantly formed and galvanized for action and within a very short space of time alternative plans were being discussed at city council level.

The interface between the church and the local community blunted the church's cutting edge. The church was not allowed to *be* the church but simply an expression of the cultural ethos in which it happened to find itself. A benign and dangerous formalism characterised by kindness and middle-class values threatened its very life. St

Wystan's had been around since Domesday but was wobbling its way into the modern world.

I thought the incumbent vicar might best be instantly forgotten at our initial meeting. His glacial intellectualism and lean, ascetic features communicated a no-go area as far as small talk and common generalities were concerned. But after a few weeks a natural lubrication of kindred spirits ensured a much easier relationship and I was able to share in the life of the worshipping community quite easily. I discovered that my 'supervisor' had a dry sense of humour. He also had a predilection for wearing a yachting cap around the village and an antipathy towards the dog collar. He survived the verbal sniping of the village diehards, pickled in traditionalism, by a combination of gritty insularity and the winning manner of his charming wife.

It was a unique experience for me and I gained valuable insight into the other life of Anglicanism. Here, there were no tipsy winos bringing their dogs and vomit into the church, no hell's angels intent on disrupting the service, no odd folk bringing their eggs and buttons up to the communion rail as a present for the vicar.

Initially I was conscious of a good deal of impatience on my part to see things happen. I asked myself more questions than I had answers for. I purposefully cultivated a certain discipline in my responses, learning to listen rather than talk. The liturgical pattern – BCP and a faint whiff of Series Two with no charismatic cream – made my brain stew in glue at times. But, most important of all, behind those chintzy curtains in the mock-Georgian houses I found that the people were much the same as anywhere else. Their problems, fears, hopes and aspirations were confided to me and the meaning of ministry became crystallized.

114

15

Fasten all Dog Collars

The last term at college was occupied with pre-ordination training and included some very off-beat pursuits such as viewing the business end of the local crematorium. All the emotional props for the bereaved were in the shop window – the syrupy vibratoes of the electronic organ, banks of flowers, stained-glass windows with a coloured vista of rolling hills and a fountain complete with cherubs spouting liquid glory in the sunshine. Beyond the view of the mourners were the ovens where the attendants reverently raked out the six and a half pounds of grey ash which was all that remained of the deceased. After viewing this we were conducted to the embalming room of an undertaker's emporium. It was a useful exercise in the gritty business of parsoneering although I must confess, it was a rather depressing week.

We also went down a coal mine and, after crawling three quarters of a mile on a two and a half foot seam, I had a sympathetic appreciation of the hazards in the mining industry and a good deal of empathy with the pit communities – which was reinforced during the subsequent strike.

The day came when I left college and it was a high peak in my life when I was presented with my diploma and the privilege of wearing the college hood. My outlook had undergone a subtle change in the twelve months I had been a student. In the senior common room, during the buffet and presentation ceremony, I no longer felt the prize buffoon but found myself conversing with an easy affability to budding bishops and donnish doctors.

There had been a good deal of discussion about my future ministry in the church. I still felt a strong call to industrial chaplaincy. My bishop was warm to this suggestion and so it was decided I should serve my title as a curate working three days a week in a parish and three days in local industry.

The penultimate stage of my pre-ordination training was a retreat which took place in a large mansion suitably buried in the countryside. Everyone behaved in a distinctly holy way and there was a sanctified cloyness about the place, which stuck.

Walking like cockroaches through the raspberry canes which bordered the garden, my black-cassocked mates took on a different identity. Silence was the order of the day. 'Please pass the salt' at meal times became an exercise in semantics and I didn't know whether I might upset the applecart if I'd have whispered a sibilant 'No' to a second helping of rice pudding. In some ways, I welcomed the silence because the struggle to establish relationships was nullified; the fuse cap was taken out of those interminable, 'What-were-you-doing-before-you-came-here' conversations. We sprawled around the common room in our cassocks looking like lost dogs waiting to be picked up by their owners. Some sat gazing at a leaflet on the wall advertising four days of Quiet Meditation and Retreat left over from the previous month.

Two enterprising characters played a zippy game of chess. Others read and the quiet frustration on their faces convinced me they were trying to read the books upside down to relieve the pressure on their brains.

The books on the shelves in the common room were designed to mould the devotional life. I looked at the titles and felt suitably mouldy. *Ninty-eight Ways to a Holy Life, Seventy-six Ways to Meditate,* and there were those volumes written by Teutonic theologiamaniacs under titles like *Eingengesetzlichkeiten* by Rudolph Broken-Sprocket. To paraphrase, like dead codfish in the candlelight, they glowed but stank. I told myself it was a lack of spirituality on my part and began to feel guilty but then picked up Sangster's *Pure in Heart* and felt something of the heat of the devotional life. I told myself that Sangster was a master craftsman, a writer who knew his stuff and my guilt began to vapourize. People like Broken-Sprocket might be pretty hot on devotion, but they were rotten writers.

I couldn't use the public telephone to call Pat. It was in the hall and I supposed one could have been executed on the spot if one were foolhardy enough to pick the thing up.

I finally had to confess to myself that I am quite helpless not being able to use verbal communication. I am heavily dependent on words. There is a place for silence in heaven – although half an hour doesn't seem long in eternity. God speaks in silence but I am a child of my age and find the noise of my own personality intrudes when it is an *imposed* silence. Even small talk, inconsequential chatter, is sometimes a necessary lubrication in social relationships. But I reflected that silence for three days isn't a bad thing, given my deaf left ear, my new false teeth and a natural shyness.

Ordination day arrived and there was an end-of-term atmosphere as the photographs were taken outside the cathedral. Friends, relatives and wellwishers posed in phalanxes of smiling sanctity.

The crunch came on Monday morning. I felt very self-conscious in my dog collar, almost embarrassed. Too many telly adverts of effete curates drinking a well-known brand of tea and nibbling arrowroots biscuits had eroded my confidence. I prefer my tea to be irony-red, strong enough to corrode the spoon, and treacle sweet. Arrowroot biscuits savour of nanny and bedtime stories. Anyway, I was learning to be a fully paid-up member of the Anglican ministry and I had to do things the proper way. Parish visiting was a high priority and here my twelve months at St Wystan's proved to be a useful ballast.

It was a nerve-racking moment when, with the full-time

industrial chaplain, I made my way through those familiar factory gates through which I had walked for thirty-three years. The dog collar felt unusually tight and my knees were wobbly. We went to the security gatehouse to present our credentials. The security chief, a man I'd known for almost forty years and whose progress I had charted from his lorry driving days to splendidly-uniformed factory policeman, looked at me – a hard, suspicious, unfriendly look.

'An' what are we supposed to call yer *now*?' he said, and the 'now' was heavily accentuated.

'Call me what you've always called me Syd,' I replied which, in the light of past experience, was a risky thing to say. Syd had always been a robust personality who expressed himself forcibly and in colourful language.

He grinned and relaxed. 'You're still bible punchin' Ralph – officially now with yer dog collar!'

'Yes. Something like that,' I replied. 'The powers that be feel that you lot need special treatment so I'm going to be your proper connecting link between this life and the next!'

Syd appreciated the humour and I was then conducted to the inner sanctuary of 'mahogany row' where the key managerial personnel were located. I was formally introduced to the works manager, a brisk, efficient rising star in the industrial firmament. We exchanged reminiscences about those times when I had been a shop steward and part of his duties as an under-manager had been to adjudicate at the appellate stage of the disciplinary procedure. It was mildly embarrassing but manageable conversational mileage.

I was very thankful I'd left a deposit of goodwill in the factory and felt immediately that my reception was warm and sympathetic. Even my old union colleagues welcomed me back with haemorrhages of goodwill. The square-wheel phraseology of some of my union mates still sounded endearingly attractive. After all, I'd seen more lights at the end of more tunnels than Galileo saw stars through his telescope. The victories for common sense that I had won eclipsed anything Napoleon ever achieved. Ongoing situations were faced even before they started and I had never once stood idly by and watched the living standards of my members erode because of many years of Tory misrule. There had been numerous times when meaningful discussions had taken place, and I'd had more than my fair share of confrontations. It was good to be back and I write about my shop floor identity like a condemned man giving an unbiased view on capital punishment.

·In retrospect, unionology had become part of my blood stream and the old problems in new guises were the talking points among the union fraternity – non-payment of irritation money for handling glass-fibre, the threat of blacking smelly urinals (there was a problem!), rats reported in the reclamation, discrepancies in overtime pay, injury benefits, the yearly pay award and so on.

Industrial chaplaincy was a ministry which attracted me like a moth to a flame. Being a product of the working class, I love the shop floor man. His candour, his impatience with humbug and hypocrisy; his cheerfulness when the cards are stacked against him; his resilience and adaptability when the necessity for change is put to him in a straightforward and fair way; his compassion for the underdog and his eternal optimism which always sees big daddy Littlewoods knocking on the door with the goodies.

The camaraderie was still there with the sick clubs, raffles for the retired, collections for the kids' Christmas party, whip rounds for the body scanner appeal – it was a secular *koinonia* I found most attractive.

Of course, according to my union friends, it was management who needed 'saving'. But then, I reasoned from the union point of view, they always did! Management on the other hand were eloquently silent regarding their relationship with the union. But then, they always were!

In the first few weeks of my ministry in the factory I

discovered little had changed in the traditional stances of union and management but there was a sharper awareness of the issues involved. Generations of rail shopmen had worked in the rail shops hardly knowing or caring what was happening in the economic world outside. The late 1970s had seen the first cold slivers of economic recession and a new word – redundancy – was being freely bandied about. Up to this time 'competition' was something to do with crosswords and football but gradually, it had come to mean something to do with railway rolling stock. Government funding was not a widow's cruse of oil – the miraculous handout, whether needed or not. A new technology was spawning new skills and I noticed startling changes taking place on the shop floor. There were new machines with banks of dials, illuminated knobs and winking lights with programmed tapes to take the place of the manual competency that had gone before; the blokes looked younger, the shops looked cleaner and smelt more acceptable.

Although there seemed to be an atmosphere of brisk efficiency there was also an underlying anxiety which transmitted a voltage of very high currency. The industry had already shed a tremendous number of jobs and the twelve BREL workshops spread over the country were rumoured to be tightening up still further. The question uppermost in the minds of management and union was, 'Where will the axe fall next?' and inevitably, this had the effect of solidifying the interests of both parties. As Dr Johnson might have put it, nothing concentrates the mind more than the possibility of 6,000 men being made redundant in a short space of time. Although no explicit recognition of a united front on the part of management-union was forthcoming, and although the bunkers continued to be manned by hard-headed sectional interests, the feeling that 'we are all in the same boat so we'd better row together' was emerging. And the economic waters were getting very choppy. In other parts of the country unemployment had ceased to be an academic headache and was becoming an accepted way of life for millions.

So, my impressions during the first few months of my chaplaincy were beginning to take shape and shortly afterwards, I was invited to go to a high-unemployment blackspot and take a look at the other face of Britain. I shall draw a veil over the exact location; suffice to say, it could have been duplicated a dozen times and I have no doubt that there were other areas probably worse off than the one I visited.

My guide was a plummy-voiced cleric with a thinning hairline, bristly beard and horn-rimmed specs – almost a caricature of the fun-figure beloved by telly lampoonists. But this bloke was tough as old boots. It was late afternoon and the youngsters were coming home from school. They looked normal kids until I reflected on the mind-boggling violence which came to the surface when they did an effective demolition job on the local school. We turned into a shopping precinct which once boasted a smart phalanx of glass and chrome frontages to washerterias, curry bars, butcher, baker and so on. Now most of the shops were locked and barred with ugly strips of corrugated iron for windows. I asked what had happened.

'Sold up, bankrupt, clapped out,' was the laconic comment. He pointed out one brightly lit store selling everything from elastic bands to butter. 'That's been broken into twenty times.'

I didn't have the heart to ask him over what period of time.

The three great factories which had once been the vital arteries supplying economic life-blood to the community, were now empty. They looked like industrial Marie Celestes. The blank spaces where the windows used to be were like leaden eyes staring at the vast open areas of ground. High rise flats (the social planners' dream and the occupants' nightmare) had been levelled to the ground. Hugging the skyline in the far distance was the large multi-national engineering concern which, local rumour had it, was soon to be shipped abroad.

Here and there human dignity had clawed out of the sombre dereliction a modicum of self respect. There were well-tended lawns and a few daffs lolling in the breeze and bowing their heads in sympathy. Some of the council houses were evidently now owned by the tenants who had revolted against the slab-faced monotony of the estate by tarting up the fronts of their houses in all kinds of architectural non-conformity. The brass knockers and letter-boxes were still brightly polished although it is a safe bet that the improvements were made before the recession.

We threaded our way through ruler-straight streets past houses which for some reason or other had had their original roofs lopped off and lowered by the council.

'That pub', said my plummy cleric, pointing to a hostelry with a swinging ark sign, 'is where the local mafia meet. Convenient for the coppers – they always know where to find the villains.'

There were other places he showed me with no trace of humour in his voice. I felt the atmosphere in the car, almost as though he had taken a suppressed sob for a stroll.

Many of the churches had given up. My friend pointed out one derelict building which had once been a place of worship but now looked like a disused barn. The walls were blackened by the habitual fires lit in the place by kids, meth men, or somebody.

'The fellow who pastored that church was a youngish chap,' he said. 'He died of a seizure brought on by the situation in which he worked.'

In another part of the area, I visited a place which dispensed comfort to the unemployed. A mixture of sound advice, encouragement and weak tea. It was a sad little building, an adjunct of the community self-help organization and had once been a Catholic school. The place was situated in a run-down area, because of the peppercorn rent I suppose.

Up two flights of stairs and on a landing was a tier of redundant filing cabinets and on the wall a 1980 calendar; the picture was pretty but dusty. I walked through a door with a notice in red biro inviting me to enter. The office was furnished in spartan fashion and the funding for the enterprise was an amalgam of local initiative. My brief was to find out what was being done for the unemployed.

Behind a desk sat a little bloke with crevices in his face – a worn out lonely-looking face which had grown old without too much time being involved. I discovered he had been employed for over twenty years by a local firm before being made redundant. His replies to my questions were well-honed and he muttered darkly about a two-nation state and Peterloo. Outside a chill wind was blowing and sweeping the streets of its old newspapers, cola cans and fag packets and the little man droned on about drop-in centres, People's March for Jobs, YTS schemes and the well-patronized local flea market.

After my time spent in Darkest England I returned to base and joined the rest of the investigative team. We had dinner followed by coffee, followed by a post-mortem under the general title, 'The Church and The Unemployed'. There was a sixty per cent unemployment problem in the area. I didn't say much. I could cope with statistics. It was the people that bothered me.

16

Back on the Shop Floor

Pat was admitted to hospital to undergo surgery for a thyroid condition and the morning after the operation I slipped out of the factory to see her. I was wearing my dog collar – an immediate passport to the hospital outside normal visiting hours.

It was a small ward catering for eight patients. Pat looked a bit under the weather and had difficulty in speaking so I whispered in her ear, said a prayer, kissed her and left. Later, that evening, I saw her again and the other patients were smiling broadly as I entered the ward. Pat was feeling much better and I asked, 'What's the joke – why are they amused?'

She laughed, 'After you left this morning the girl in the next bed said, 'My word, you *have* got a friendly vicar – fancy him kissing you like that!' and I replied, 'I've been married to my friendly vicar for thirty-four years!'

The moral of that little story is: what we see isn't necessarily the sum total of the truth. So, in the same way, there have been occasions on the factory floor, especially when breaking new ground, when the workforce has been under the mistaken impression that because I wear a dog collar I'm a stranger to life on the shop floor! Of course, nothing could be further from the truth and the sooner that's clear, the sooner I can get on with the job.

Industrial mission is a comparative newcomer to the Church's outreach. The principle of appointing chaplains grew up during and immediately after the Second World War, the underlying motive being that 'if the people won't come to the Church, the Church must go to the people'. It is an ecumenical undertaking. The factory is no respecter of denominations or doctrinal hobby-horses. A fanatical Methodist or Baptist or Anglican or United Reformed churchman will have an identity crisis as far as the factory is concerned. For the average working man the dog collar represents a steeple, a robed choir, a liturgy and all the trappings of tradition. For his part, the chaplain's concern is for everyone in the place, from the top management to the canteen washer-upper. He is a guest, not on the payroll, and is unaffected by policy decisions in the work situation. It is considered infra dig for him to air the problems of the factory in public, for example, if the company has interests in South African banking, then it would be discourteous and self-defeating to enjoy the luxury of making adverse press comments. After all, if one is a guest in someone's home, one doesn't criticize the cooking. A certain degree of trust must be maintained.

An industrial dispute raises the temperature on both sides and if it reaches flashpoint, then a strike is on the cards, and the responsibility of resolving the problem lies entirely within the parties involved. The chaplain will inevitably be drawn into it. Both union and management will solicit his views and there will certainly be keen discussion of the issues involved around the mashing can during the mid-morning 'snap'. But at all times the chaplain's stance must be one of non-alignment. He will always be a reconciler, always a promoter and searcher for social justice and good relationships.

I am often asked 'What's the difference between a committed Christian worker employed by the factory and an industrial chaplain?' One of the differences is that the chaplain has *carte blanche* to go anywhere and talk to anyone – subject to common courtesies – in the industrial setting. This access is hierarchical and geographical and nobody else in the factory has this privilege. There is an enormous potential here but parallel with the potential is the responsibility it carries. When men and women open up their hearts to me about the most sensitive and secret things in their lives, then that confidentiality is as sacred as the confessional. The workforce rightly expects my lips to be sealed, even when the euphoric atmosphere of the Works Manager's Christmas party threatens the chaplain's code of working practice!

The chaplain is not owned by the firm and if he's sensible, he'll reject the offer of an office or counselling room. Having no 'role' he must be seen to be completely independent of outside pressures so any counselling is done off-site. Compared to many others in the factory, the chaplain is powerless, but precisely because he is outside the system his influence is greater than he is sometimes aware.

A particularly rewarding and humbling area of ministry is when I am called to make regular off-site visits to employees suffering from a terminal illness.

Bill was always a cheerful character and at sixty, was looking forward to possible early redundancy with a handsome lump sum because the firm was short of orders and laying off staff. One day I was asked by the personnel manager to visit Bill because he had recently undergone hospital tests and the findings were not hopeful. Stomach cancer had been diagnozed.

I went to the small terraced house where Bill was lying on a settee-cum-bed. His wife, a chirpy, courageous woman fussed around him badgering him to make haste and get well 'because the darts team at the Barley Mow were short of their star player'. When she looked at me her eyes mirrored all the anxiety and tension of the situation.

'Bill's always cheerful,' she said simply.

Bill looked at the battery of tablets on the table. 'The pills make me happy,' he joked, with a wry smile.

Over the next few weeks I made my regular visits and Bill's wife took the opportunity to do some shopping while I sat with him. We talked about life and death, we laughed about some of the characters he'd worked with and as the weeks went by, his condition worsened and he became emaciated and incontinent.

At the conclusion of my visits, we always had a word of prayer and Bill looked forward to this time; it was a very precious and hallowed moment when we prayed together. On my last visit, his wife and two married daughters were present and Bill murmured, 'We're having some prayer, aren't we?'

'Of course,' I replied, 'let's join hands.'

I prayed a simple prayer asking God to give Bill courage to face the future. Suddenly he began to weep – which was quite out of character – and motioned for us to leave the room. As we were going out of the door his wife whispered, 'He wants you to go back'.

I returned and sat beside him cradling his head in my lap. He was still sobbing so I tried to comfort him but suddenly he looked at me.

His eyes were shining and he said, 'These aren't tears of sorrow or fear Ralph, they're tears of joy!' and he actually laughed.

Three days later he died. I conducted his funeral. It was a most moving experience because when I got to the words, 'Death, where is thy sting? Grave where is thy victory?' I felt I had seen a living exposition of the resurrection power of the living Christ.

In order to build individual relationships with folk like Bill, it is essential to *meet* them. I try to meet people at all levels but very often, my main area of difficulty is the sheer logistics of covering a 200-acre site with 2,500 employees working a three shift system. For example, I presented my credentials at one huge factory and was asked if I had brought my bike clips.

'Why?' I replied.

'Because if you can't ride a bike then you'd better get a pair of stout walking shoes.'

Fortunately I have never got rid of my Mark One stout Rudge bicycle and I did have a pair of bike clips so the next time I visited the site I was given charge of a battered single speed machine with a wobbly front wheel ('Don't worry, it knows which way to turn at mashing time!') and a chain with links that were joined by bits of wire. I was advised not to put too much pressure on the pedals.

On my first trip I did a rough imitation of a circus clown balanced on a one wheel contraption and the chain snapped.

'What's up?' enquired a bloke pushing a barrow.

'My chains fell off,' I said.

'As long 'as yer 'eart's free I shouldn't worry,' he gurgled.

I marked him down as a jokey character with Wesleyan connections and made a mental note to cultivate his friendship.

As well as actually getting around, another main objective of my factory visits is to develop as broad a view as possible about the firm. What does it make? Has it a diversity of operations? Is it part of a group? How many people are employed? Overseas markets? Profitability? Future planning? And so on. So I am careful to include in my weekly contacts people from every level of the organization. Introductions and explanations are channels by which relationships are established.

Very often I am called upon to talk to YTS trainees and I find this particularly difficult. It is hard to look into the eyes of a sixteen year old and see the expectation of a job he might have had, disappearing. He very often resents a society which has prepared him for a job all through his school years and then lets him down with a bump at the critical point. It is a hard pill to swallow and many YTS people regard their stint on the shop floor as a cross between cheap labour and a palliative for the real thing.

There is an ingrained assumption among some on the shop floor that my function in the factory is as a kind of moral policeman.

Not only do they regard me as the custodian of Absolutes, but also as the executor of all the absolute values. Vicars do not laugh at dirty jokes, have rows, experience trouble with mothers-in-law, pinch office pencils, spit in the street, ogle attractive girls, lose their tempers, have doubts about God, feel tetchy, booze, gamble, swear . . . In other words, vicars are slightly more than human because they are God's reps. They feed on angels' food and clock in and out of heaven. In fact, in the eyes of many of the shop floor fraternity the parson isn't regarded as salty but *soppy*. They would almost certainly agree with Ibsen's assessment, spoken in the person of the Emperor Julian. 'Have you looked at these Christians closely?' he writes. 'Hollow-eyed, pale-cheeked flat-breasted all; they brood their lives away unspurred by ambition; the sun shines for them, but they do not see it; the earth offers them its fullness but they desire it not; all their desire is to renounce and to suffer that they may come to die.' Oliver Wendell Holmes once said, 'I might have entered the ministry if certain clergymen I knew had not looked and acted like undertakers.' And Robert Louis Stevenson wrote in his diary as if it was newsworthy, 'I have been to church today and am not depressed.' Now, these examples could be multiplied and they represent a picture of monochrome vapidity.

So often, the chap with the dog collar in the factory is slotted into the category reserved for him. Any chaplain who feels he can make a mark with the men by adopting what he might feel to be a matey, no-nonsense approach will also be a-slumming at his peril. The blokes can smell a phoney a mile away and the smell is as powerful as the stench of a skunk. So it is as well to declare lines of demarcation. I don't laugh at dirty jokes because I respect wives, daughters and girl friends – my mother-in-law was a gem. I don't swear because the first thing God did when he saved me was to give me a good mouthwash. And so on. Working men respect straight explanations and declared standards.

Even so, over and over again I stumbled across the old, worn-down, preconceived ideas about parsons – and not just on the shop floor. Like the time, a few years ago, when Pat and me went to Boscombe for our annual holiday. One balmy sunny evening we sat on a form looking out to sea, bathing our thoughts in that special magic conjured up by memories, the sea air and spare time.

Suddenly I heard a voice say, 'Bin a nice day, ain't it?' and there stood a little man with a face like a lived-in bed, a walrus moustache and well-greased hair. His wife was an ample lady with skinny cobwebs underneath her eyes. They seated themselves on the form beside us.

We exchanged pleasantries and then his wife said in an injured voice, 'We went to Malta last year – first time we 'bin abroad an' it'll be the last.'

'Never agen,' the little man echoed.

'Fed us on funny fish,' his wife continued. 'Octupuses some of it was. An' Malta is infested with religion an' priests.'

'Honest?' I asked unbelievingly.

'True as we sit 'ere,' nodded the little man.

The conversation went flat while we digested the funny fish and infestation of priests and at length I broke the silence by asking him, 'What's your job?'

'Worked in a foundry for forty-seven years,' he replied. 'Now I'm retired. Live in Sheffield. What's your line of work?'

'You're not going to believe me,' I said cautiously. 'I'm a priest!'

He laughed 'Garn – you must be jokin'!'

His laughter was infectious because his wife began to laugh, great gusty, gutsy paeons of belly gurgles. 'Pull the other one,' she said, wiping the tears from her eyes.

'Aye – pull t'other,' spluttered the little man. 'Vicars talk *posh*. Not like you. You don't *sound* like a vicar.'

Pat leaned over and in a sapphire-sincere voice said, 'It's true.'

The little man stopped chortling, 'Do you sing in one of the la-di-dah voices like them blokes in Malta?'

'No. I'm a bread-and-butter bloke.'

The conversation died. The four of us sat hogging the skyline when suddenly the little man stood up and said, 'C'mon Lil. We got to go.' He turned to me and apologetically smiled, ''Ope we didn't offend you – them priests in Malta . . . '

'Not a bit' I replied. 'Only next time you see a priest, remember, he's just like you.'

'Cept 'e goes to church,' he nodded.

'Something like that,' I replied.

So, again, the idea that vicars are a different *kind* of person comes to the surface. Working as a chaplain in industry, I want to dissolve this preconception and get the men to see me for what I really am – a bread-and-butter bloke like them.

It's different from working with a congregation. In industry I meet 'man in his strength'. I have no excuse for being on the shop floor; there is no acknowledged need for my presence in the factory. I am not ministering to the sick or the old. Sometimes this may make my job more difficult, but I look at it this way – I don't have to discover a man in need before I relate effectively to him. And the real joy is actually being on the factory floor (not trapped in some cosy little office) so that I can see what they see, hear what they hear and know what they know. How else could I influence their lives? We can't speak the truth in a void; neither can it be comprehended in a void.

I have now had the opportunity of looking at industry from two very different perspectives – as a shop floor man and as an establishment figure looking in. There has been a growing understanding on my part of the social consequences of man's involvement in industry, and what is beginning to emerge is a ministry with a two-fold thrust. There is a ministry of encouragement – getting men to see their work as part of a whole and not as an end in itself;

131

sharing with them the burden of uncertainties, pressures and tensions of life in the plant. There is also the prophetic ministry – helping people to realize ends rather than means and setting their goals in a broader perspective as part of a group, so that men can see for themselves what is worthy and what is not.

Your average worker in the factory takes a static view of the world and sees himself as flotsam, heaving and pitching on an ocean of outside influences over which he has no control. He feels himself to be at the mercy of the union policy-makers in Transport House, the decision-makers in Whitehall, the managerial dictates in the factory. Getting men to ask questions, to recognize what is good and what is evil, to be discontented with the status quo and suggest workable and worthwhile alternatives – these are some of the issues involved in the chaplain's prophetic role.

Because I am the recognized 'God-man' in the place, my judgement is very often sought as the last word in any private difficulty. The bureaucratic bumbledom of our complex society confuses and distresses many ordinary folk when bereavement or redundancy strikes. I can act as a bridge between specialized helping agencies in the local community and the man in need of advice. In those factories where the welfare facilities are handled by the personnel department, a man is sometimes embarrassed by having to air his personal problems to someone within the same organization. In such cases the chaplain is strategically placed to offer a helping hand and put him in touch with a competent band of people who can help. A wise referral is a godsend to people in trouble and is certainly not a pastoral failure.

I do more listening than talking in my job and I shall always be indebted to Anne Long who lectured on Pastoral Care at St John's. I never knew what the art of listening was until Anne opened up the subject. Words, tone, speech, silence, tears, pace, body posture, dress – all are 'heard' in listening. The value of the listening ministry is that thoughts are shaped and clarified, emotions are ventilated and support can be experienced. Perhaps most important of all, the person who is being heard knows he has value. There is a discipline in the art. Tedious and boring people always irritate me and I have a tendency to focus my interest on the wallpaper; yet the bloke who appears to be as interesting as a newly-painted barn door might be the very person God wants me to listen to for very good reasons.

Time is a precious commodity – any time – but when someone is in trouble they don't want me to take crafty glances at my watch. My business is eternity rather than time; whether I have five minutes or a hundred and fifty, they must feel relaxed.

Many folk on the shop floor find difficulty in articulating deep and personal problems. They get bogged down and start talking in circles and at that point, I find it useful to gently ask a question to lubricate the process. I don't try to fill silence with words, there's always something happening in the silences anyway. Even tears talk.

17

Wake Up, the Service is Over!

When inevitably I was sent on a course to be initiated into the deeper mysteries of industrial mission, I thought I had some idea of the format. However, I found this was not so. All my preconceived ideas took a nose dive. The course tutors were not immediately identifiable as Christian ministers in the orthodox sense. Rather, they looked like a disgruntled and dishevelled crowd of civil servants, and there was an air of desperation about the company — fag smoke furiously puffed betrayed an underlying frustration.

The puffer-in-chief used grimy phrases like 'shop floor argot,' to reinforce a point and there was a tendency among the company to out-grime each other. I found it a valuable exercise to note the dynamics at work — pitched rather lower than that bit in the New Testament about whatever things are pure etcetera.

At the first session we kicked around the question, 'Would Jesus qualify for SAS or SPG elitism?' This was raised by a grizzled youngster with a grey beard, yak-like mane and deep corrugations in his brow. His ideas were cantered out like racehorses on a morning sprint. I could tell he'd done this kind of thing before. It was, in Shakespeare's matchless economy of wordy-wisdom, much ado about nothing.

When discussion somehow slithered into the international arena, words like Solidarity, Liberation Theology and Nicaragua began to assume fearful proportions. These all had something to do with negotiating learning contracts.

Then the hatchet man cometh, a thin bloke looking like the woodcut of an undernourished Mohican. To this day, I'm convinced that his brain was in imminent danger of packing up altogether due to the sheer volume of options open to him, something the Latin calls *obscurum um per obscurius*. There is a point in all these situations when a mental cut-off mercifully lowers the temperature of my critical mass, and I pass out mentally.

At last the summer-up appeared on the scene. He said he'd crystallized everything with three W's: What Went Well and What Went Wong. No doubt he meant 'Wrong' but by this time my deaf aid was beginning to play up, and I swear he said 'Wong' because everybody laughed. He was the joker in the pack – he wanted to know what value the session had been.

The evening group consisted of nine men being jollied along by a posh-speaking cleric from Suburbotopia. On his right hand was a cold fish, alleged to be a factory manager who was also a bit of a dab hand at theology and was pursuing some Bishop's Certificate. I'd have given him one right away just to see if he could smile. On the clergyman's left sat a little man with bulbous eyes filling pebble-specs. He was a works convenor – the only non-church affiliated member of the group and obviously very uncomfortable. He had been invited to make up the deficiency in working-class numbers and sat quietly, deferentially, while Latin America, Liberation Theology and the Church of Rome was being aired.

I instantly warmed to him. I think I know what was going on in his mind: this was a world of middle-class values where they were dealing with abstract, propositional language which is totally foreign to the shop floor.

Semantic tools in the factory have a dreariness, a drudging monotony that reflects something of the environment. The four-letter word which is used as an adjective, adverb, noun, verb and can be endlessly manipulated to fit any application, still remains the fundamental means of articulation on the shop floor. Indeed, some men would find it genuinely difficult to express themselves if this were not so.

The *Sun* and *Mirror* are instant news. 'Gotcha!' the screaming headline in the *Sun* after the sinking of the Belgrano is understandable, emotive and colourful; Princess Di, Charles, Philip, Anne and the Queen Mum are warm, affectionate folks – just like you and me; yobs, slobs and gobs are onomatopoeic heart warmers. The Church cannot afford to ignore this cultural divide. The two minute Godspot on early morning local radio is another example. A smooth, word-perfect homily with no rough edges is good radio but, paradoxically, poor material for gripping the attention of slingers, millwrights, labourers and bosh-borers when they are hurrying to get ready for work.

The working class thinks in picture language. The visual has an immediacy that short-circuits what others may feel are superior modes of communication. Russell Harty has the edge on Richard Hoggart, Wogan is easier on the eye and the ear than Wittgenstein.

Most of our church services are designed to accommodate a literary congregation of articulate people. If a working class person is persuaded to pay a visit to St Whatsit's the first thing that happens is that a pile of books is shoved in his hand – an *ASB,* a *Mission Praise* hymnbook or a *Hymns Ancient and Modern,* a service sheet and a *Good News Bible*. Then he'll feel mentally raped when the vicar says at the beginning of the service, 'Turn to your neighbour, shake his or her hand and wish them "Good morning".' There are a lot of quiet people in our churches who want to be part of an anonymous congregation and are happy to be lost in the crowd until, in God's good time, they are found. But in the liturgical strait-jacket, even the slight thaw of a structured jolly greeting isn't sufficient to warm the cockles of a cold heart. Indeed, when a church is a cemetery of hats and memories on a wet Sunday night in February and one senses the refusal of those grey stones and grey people to lend themselves to experimentation in worship, my heart bleeds for the young priest who has grown ten years older in the first year of his five-year appointment.

There is a great deal of work to be done in improving the image of the Church, and of the C of E in particular, especially in the area of ministry in which I am involved. It is true that many of our inner-city churches have responded to the need and have shaped their services to incorporate and accept people who have a different cultural tradition to the one normally associated with Anglicanism. Indeed, some churches have made tremendous strides. But I believe that others are sick with a terminal illness and dying with gracious dignity.

One only has to read the letters column of the *Daily Telegraph* to sense the hurt and dismay of venerable members of the Anglican Church at the passing of the *BCP* and the coming of the new liturgies. Like Jonah in the whale, these good people have a right to be incorporated but not assimilated. I accept their burning sincerity but if our Church is to have any meaning or relevance to modern man, then we must critically examine the structures.

The Church is described in the New Testament as a body and studying the health of the body – whether good or bad – is a legitimate pursuit. The Church is not a static institution. Indeed, the words used to describe it are organic not institutional, and since some churches are going and growing, while others are crying and dying, we can't attribute these conditions to merely sociological changes. The fault lies in ourselves. An hour's walk through a factory complex would surely convince members of the Prayer Book Society that if the Church is to *be* the Church it must have an intelligible message to present to the world. It is not intelligible to talk of Sexagesima and Quinquagesima. An ordinary bloke might think these are new aftershave lotions. 'Obviously, we don't *talk* in this kind of language,' may come the reply. But the identifiable strain is there even when we talk of going to Matins and Evensong.

I suggest that words lose their impact and meaning becomes dulled through repetition and so, to repeat the same formula year in and year out has a tendency to blunt the spiritual sensitivity. A scaffolding for worship is right and proper but when the scaffolding becomes the building itself, it is simply grotesque.

Industrial man, especially on the assembly line, faces an everyday problem of the eight-hour schedule where things are done in the right order with no margin for error. His brain floats free from the dull mechanistic activity but it is the freedom which comes from always running away from the dull reality of his job. That's why when he's finished his work for the day he turns his mind to the things that are really satisfying and fulfilling like gardening, beekeeping and fishing. 'Ah,' says the critic, 'but isn't work meant to be part of that total fulfilment?' It is – but try to get the man that does a dirty, repetitive job to see the truth of this. He *needs* the resources of the Church, but if the shop window of the 6.30 Evensong exhibits the boring, plodding predictability of liturgmania at its most narcophilic, then he'll look elsewhere for answers.

We have come a long way since the early twenties when an edition of *Hymns Ancient and Modern* contained a hymn, 'For a Service of Working Men':

> Sons of Labour dear to Jesus
> To your homes and work again;
> Go with brave hearts back to duty,
> Face the peril, bear the pain.

It was obviously a hymn designed to stiffen the backbone of the working man and give him a jut-jawed dedication to the Protestant Work Ethic. He had to like it or lump it. If he was fed up with his two up and two down house then hymn No. 586 gave him food for thought:

Be your dwelling ne'er so lowly,
    Yet remember, by your bed,
That the Son of God most holy
    Had not where to lay his head.

We acquired a lot of our religion from the Greeks and like the Greek statuary in our museums, it is cold, lifeless and half its limbs are missing. It is cerebral. In the Church of England we have a problem with our bodies. The Greeks didn't reckon much to fleshly bodies – they need a lot of maintenance, are somehow dirty and subject to decay. To the Jews however, the body was indispensable in manifesting the deepest emotional feelings to Jahweh. The Wailing Wall in Jerusalem is a sight to behold at a barmitzvah or Succoth. The shalom of God can only be expressed through a liberated body and so the Jew will pray with his body as well as his lips. The Hasidic Jew especially finds release in using his body to worship his Creator. For the most part, in Anglicanism, we're a bit embarrassed with all this. We need to rediscover the Jewish roots of our worship.

I find that taking an eight a.m. 1662 Communion Service is particularly painful. The congregation are like tight little islands of self-sufficiency, kneeling in total seclusion from each other. When the minister appears, they sink even lower – as though he's about to mow the lot down with an AK 47. If someone should show any emotion by vocalizing his happy acceptance of what the preacher says by a muted 'Amen', then it won't be interpreted as a sign of revival, but somebody disturbing the service, or possibly the congregation may feel some poor wretch has religious mania.

So when the shop floor fraternity – even regular communicants among them – tell me they find Anglican services 'dull', then it is time we asked some fundamental questions. Why do we accept a format of worship which many feel is insulting to God and man by its sheer mediocrity? What have we been doing in the last hour and a quarter at the 6.30 Evensong? Why am I here, sitting in what appears to be a liturgical warehouse of bits and pieces collected over the centuries? What is the vision of this community? Is the Church truly what is left if the building collapses? Would it make any difference if the Holy Spirit vacated this particular church . . . ?

The Archbishop's Report on urban priority areas reinforces the view that we are seriously lacking in our response to the liturgical needs of our inner-city churches. We should all pay particular attention to the section headed 'Worship'.

18

Dissatisfied Satisfaction

I am conscious of so many contradictions in my life; subtle changes in my thinking and attitudes. Yet this is entirely in keeping with the progress of God's grace in dealing with the human personality. It is a process of refinement. The crucible of God's testing is sometimes painful, often frustrating, but never without meaning or purpose.

Nowadays, when people say to me, 'Having worn more than one cap, in your post-war working life, and now being ordained, have you "arrived"? Are you fulfilled?' I must answer 'No'. As an American General philosophically commented, when writing about war, 'War is another hill, and beyond the hill, a river, and beyond the river, another hill . . . '

In the final analysis we shall never be fulfilled until we reach the end of the pilgrimage, and that finishes in heaven. Until then, we may continue to honk the Good News in any factory which invites us into its workshops. Change is a built-in component, a permanent feature of life itself, so it is no surprise that there are contradictions.

As a full time industrial chaplain, my ministry takes me into the factories of major employers with household names – Rolls Royce, British Rail, Courtauld's . . . but as I began my post-war working life in British Rail workshops it is there where I can gauge the changes. We have moved a long way in Derby since the Midland Railway set up its headquarters in 1844. In those days the works had three messrooms, one being fitted with a rostrum and an organ. There, local clergy held a short service for the workforce at breakfast time (in those days, starting time was 6 a.m.).

There were places for 700 men, and a spare seat was hard to find. Nowadays, if the Archangel Gabriel was to conduct an evangelistic campaign, with miracles being performed daily and raising the dead thrown in, I guess the blokes would still prefer to play dominoes and discuss fishing prospects during their lunch break.

Paradoxically, they *are* concerned about fundamental issues. They ask the basic questions which are variations on a well-known foursome: Who am I? Why am I here? Where do I come from? Where am I going? In one afternoon, a colleague was asked all the following questions:

'What about the evils perpetrated in the name of Christ?'

'What is the meaning of baptism?'

'Were Adam and Eve historical figures?'

'Does evolution prove that the Bible is a fairy story?'

'Why did the Church tolerate slavery for centuries?'

'Why is the Church always on the side of the ruling class?'

'Why doesn't the Church stand out against nuclear arms?'

'Why do bishops bless nuclear submarines?'

'What is your opinion of John Allegro's *The Sacred Mushroom and the Cross?*'

'Why are church people such hypocrites?'

'Why can't the Church do more to help the unemployed?'

'What about abortion?'

'What about the Church owning all that wealth?'

Those questions were not manufactured to solicit some kind of feedback by the chaplain – they were quite spontaneously addressed to the dog collar.

Industrial mission is not so much a frontier ministry as a foreign mission. And this mission operates in an area where a good many people spend a third of their lives. 'Go into the world and preach the gospel' includes the factory with all its problems, anxieties and, at times, its very elemental outlook on life.

I see my ministry as an extension of the cross, when the institutionalized Church as represented by the dog collar steps through the factory gates and becomes vulnerable. There it meets secular man on his own ground. *He* sets the agenda and the Church is get-attable. Sometimes the confrontation can be painful. Like my colleague who was asked the questions, I sometimes feel like a trailing socket where men can plug in for positive answers, or find some consolation in times of bereavement and those emotional earthquakes that hit the soul. Very often the questions are insoluble and I have to say, 'I don't know'. Yet somehow this gives people the assurance that the Church has a human face as well as a divine. God uses such admissions of weakness – not failures – to measure up to the secular world and its expectations; they are part of his creative process. The plugged-in parson often feels physically and emotionally drained at the end of his stint in the factory. But he doesn't knock-off at the end of the shift. There are follow-ups: hospital and sick visits, redundancy counselling and a whole host of other pastoral commitments.

On some occasions I feel like a lightning conductor. There is a lot of static in the human heart and where there's a litmus paper of frustration and the union and management look as though they are about to lock horns *and* the metaphors become as mixed as the motives, then the chaplain is there to take the surge of anger and sense of injustice.

A *trailing socket,* a *lightning conductor* and then a *generator*. I am often asked how free I am to propagate the faith. Obviously, I don't go padding round the factory with my tongue hanging out looking for potential converts. There is such a thing as pastoral lust. If I look on the workforce as a captive congregation then I shall miss the whole point. This is not the basis of my appointment. I am there to listen, to share, to learn, and also to inform the rest of the Church. My acceptance by the men is on the basis of my role as a Christian minister and a recognition that the Christian values are still the norm of our society, however much that norm is under attack. It is the Christian values and their relevance to the quality of life in that particular factory that must be my concern.

As I mentioned, men are asking deep questions and they don't expect a Christian minister like me to fob them off with platitudes of sociological or philosophical speculation. I am reminded of the melancholy lines of the First World War chaplain-poet, Studdert Kennedy.

Woodbine Willie

They gave me this name like their nature,
Compacted of laughter and tears,
A sweet that was born of the bitter,
A joke that was torn from the years

Of their travail and torture, Christ's fools,
Atoning my sins with their blood,
Who grinned in their agony sharing
The glorious madness of God.

Their name! Let me hear it – the symbol
Of unpaid – unpayable debt,
For the men to whom I owed God's Peace,
I put off with a cigarette.

I don't want to put men off. I interpret the faith against a man's background, as Jesus did – simply, directly – and I don't try to hide behind mysterious biblical or theological language. The opportunities to engage men at something deeper than threshold evangelism become more frequent as relationships become established. It takes time, patience and a lot of humour.

It's true that my brain hit a pothole when that security chief snarled, 'What are we supposed to call you now?' But going back through those gates seemed perfectly normal. I just felt as though I'd been on another course and I suppose in a way, I had. I certainly did not feel I'd 'arrived', being newly ordained, but the gates didn't seem to be as narrow as they were in 1979.

I no longer feel uncomfortable in my dog collar. In fact, there are now times when I find it a valuable help rather than a hindrance. A dog collar identifies, nobody is under any illusions; that's important on the shop floor. We can start talking without any shadow boxing. The dog collar is a role identi-kit.

I sometimes ask myself who I represent in the factory. God? The Church? Myself? More importantly, who do the blokes on the shop floor think I represent? Management? The institutionalized Church of England can't stun-gun a man into accepting all that the dog collar represents, but the priestly role *is* being fulfilled. He's got to detect the image of Christ in me, and that is a terrifying responsibility.

Doxa ('glory' in the Greek) has the meaning of 'reputation' and when Paul writes about 'glory in the Church' he means that God's reputation is revealed to the world through his Church. That's where the dog collar helps.

These days when I walk on to the shop floor on Monday mornings and those familiar sights, sounds and smells assault my senses, I sometimes feel I'm a mobile bucket-shop of cut price culture. When I was at St John's, in order to maintain my respectability, I always made sure the wordology department of my brain was well-stocked and kept up to date. I had a mental rack containing lockjaw examples of my craft in the essay-constructing section – all in alphabetical order. Antinomianism, Bultmann, Cosmology, Dada, Epistemology, Existentialism, Impressionism, Logical Posivitism, Methodology, Nihilism, and so on. But nowadays, this mental stack is collecting dust because I find them quite useless. Indeed, much of what happens in church on Sunday has little relevance to what happens the next day. Monday morning can be a bit of a let down after the heady atmosphere of a charismatic service on Sunday evening but somehow, I tell myself, I have to bridge the gap. The shop floor is my parish and the rum-looking bunch of blokes is my cure of souls. They want something more than a mere propagation of a social gospel. Jesus as some kind of Holy Beveridge doesn't register high in the conversational stakes around the mashing can at 9.30 a.m. and liberation theology has a sniff about it that inevitably fogs the real issues.

So, I return to the question, 'Have you finally "arrived"? Are you fulfilled?' and I must confess, I have a dissatisfied satisfaction. To quote the wise words of a saint in the Middle Ages — he may well have been a middle-aged saint — 'There is no stopping place in this life, nor was there ever one; always be ready for the gifts of God, especially the new ones.'

Life is a constant surprise and I often feel like a child eagerly awaiting those new and unexpected gifts that God has laid up. As Augustine of Hippo reminded us, 'The child that I was remained within me, for where else would he have gone?'

And no child is satisfied with the status quo.

More Books from Triangle

Jim Wallis
Agenda for Biblical People

A thought-provoking book, setting out a spiritual, and practical strategy for people who wish to be fully biblical in the personal, political and economic areas of their lives.

'Jim Wallis is an important voice that Christians badly need to hear . . .'   *The Rev Dr Charles Elliott*

Margaret Cundiff
Called to be Me

Lively reminiscences of a deaconess in a Yorkshire parish. With line illustrations.

'Realistic and hilarious.'   *Christian Bookseller*

Margaret Cundiff
Following On

Another enjoyable invitation to meet the people who share in the life of this busy woman minister. With line illustrations.

More Books from Triangle

Margaret Cundiff
I'd Like You to Meet . . .

And wherever she meets them – broadcasting studio, supermarket, London bus or in her parish – all have enriched her life. Here she passes that richness on.

'Margaret Cundiff is communicating God's love and joyousness all the time.' *C of E Newspaper*

Margaret Cundiff
Living By the Book

'If everybody lived by the Sermon on the Mount,' said the man on the train, 'the world would be a better place.' This remark started Margaret Cundiff on a journey of exploration to rediscover those chapters of St Matthew's Gospel which we think we know so well. Is it possible to live by the Book?

'For her, the greatest sin is to make Jesus dull'.
C of E Newspaper

Peter Mullen
Rural Rites

Tales from the fictional Yorkshire village of Marton-on-t'Moor, seen through the eyes of its much-harassed vicar.

More Books from Triangle

Peter Mullen
Country Matters

A further look at the high spirited antics of life at Marton.

'. . . may earn him the title "the James Herriot of the Church of England".' *Radio Oxford*

Brenda Courtie
Not Quite Heaven

A heart-warming account by a Liverpool housewife of deepening Christian experience through everyday life.

'Touching, funny, illuminating and unflinchingly honest.' *C of E Newspaper*

Brenda Courtie
Jenny's Year

A candid portrayal of the time-honoured role of the vicar's wife in a busy urban parish.

'The kind of animated sitcom which keeps pages turning apace...' *The Church times*

More Books from Triangle

Eric Liddell

The Disciplines of the Christian Life

The first British publication of this newly discovered work
by the hero of *Chariots of Fire*. A practical guide to
Christian living.

Morris Maddocks

Journey to Wholeness

The author considers the journey we should all take for
our personal well-being – the road leading to health,
healing and wholeness – and shows Christian healing to be
an essential element in the reconciliation of creation to the
Creator.

'This is a scholarly, well-written and convincing book that
can do nothing but good.' *Church Times*

David Adam

The Edge of Glory

Modern prayers in the Celtic tradition, written by a vicar
for daily use in his country parish in North Yorkshire.
With line illustrations.

'It is a style that beautifully combines God's glory with
everyday events.' *Christian Family*

'Lovely Celtic symbols illuminate the text'. *Church Times*

More Books from Triangle

Per-Olof Sjogren
The Jesus Prayer

This, one of the most ancient prayers of the Christian
Church, has a new meaning for people today. It remains
especially appropriate amid the busyness and anxiety of
the twentieth century.

R. M. French (translator)
The Way of a Pilgrim

A classic of Russian spirituality, which reveals new
insights into prayer.

'It has been for many, as it was for me when I read it in my
late teens, a revelation about the life of prayer.'
Metropolitan Anthony

R. M. French (translator)
The Pilgrim Continues His Way

In this sequel to *The Way of a Pilgrim*, the unknown writer
narrates his further travels to the holy places of Russia, and
becomes involved in deep discussion with a priest
concerning the nature of prayer.